MW01194186

Teaching Overseas: An Insider's Perspective

Kent Blakeney PhD

Copyright © 2016 Kent M Blakeney

All rights reserved.

ISBN: 1537533061

ISBN-13: 978-1537533063

DEDICATION

Insert dedication text here. Insert dedication text here. Insert dedication text here. Insert dedication text here. Insert dedication text here. Insert dedication text here. Insert dedication text here. Insert dedication text here. Insert dedication text here. Insert dedication text here.

CONTENTS

Africa-Middle East-Southeast Asia-South Asia-East Asia

Teacher Time

ACKNOWLEDGMENTS

This book could not have been written without the support and guidance of all the administrators and colleagues I have worked with over the past fifteen years. Their insight, experience, and passion for teaching are invaluable for students around the globe. I would also like to thank Ken Maguire for editing this edition. He had some of the best suggestions and went well beyond the call of duty to make sure the book is accurate, informative, and easy to read. Thanks Ken!!

Foreword

Over the past fifteen years I have been living overseas and teaching in six schools on four continents. I have had the best experiences of my life as well as some of the most challenging ones. Overall, it has been amazing. I love travelling and stepping outside my comfort zone. I have visited dozens of countries and experienced life inside other cultures. Highlights include taking a seven-day trip down the Coco River between Nicaragua and Honduras in a dugout canoe, meeting my future wife on a beach in Morocco, and visiting Angkor Wat in Cambodia. At the same time, there have been occasions when I felt lonely, isolated, and wanting a home-cooked meal from my mom.

In the next few paragraphs, I want to share with you a bit about me and familiarize you with the perspective I will be presenting in this book.

I began my overseas experience by volunteering in the Peace Corps. I taught environmental science to elementary school children in three small villages outside the town of El Sauce, Nicaragua. While there, I interviewed and received a position teaching social studies at the American Nicaraguan School in the capital, Managua. After one year, I moved to Morocco, where I met my wife, who is a Foreign Service Officer in the U.S. State Department. Since getting married, we have lived in Nepal, Austria, Madagascar, and Senegal.

All of my overseas education experience has been in capital cities, which is a big difference from my Peace Corps days of living in a village in the middle of nowhere with a small monthly stipend to serve my basic needs. It took two hours of riding in a converted American school bus on bumpy dirt roads to get to the nearest bank. While I sometimes long for the simplicity of my Peace Corps experiences, I do enjoy living in countries with access to 'luxuries' like air conditioning, the Internet, grocery stores, and restaurants.

My professional experience and skills have definitely improved and helped me secure jobs. When I began teaching in Managua, I had a Bachelor of Science in Education, a Bachelor of Arts in History, three years of middle school experience in North Carolina, and two years living in Nicaragua. Since then, I've added a Master's in Education from Walden University and a Ph.D. in Leadership in Education Administration from Capella University. My dissertation focused on traditional and cyber bullying in overseas middle schools. I started a research website called Overseas School Research that I hope to expand in the coming years. Beyond my education, I have completed IB and AP summer courses for educators and presented at several international school conferences. In essence, I have tried to make myself an expert in overseas education.

My perspective on writing this book is simple. Over the past several years, hundreds of people have asked me about my experiences and what it is like to teach overseas. Naturally, some have been teachers in the United States looking for a change of pace. I have always wondered why there is not a book dedicated to teaching overseas. After all, there are thousands of schools and tens of thousands of overseas teachers around the world. My goal is to provide a synopsis of overseas teaching and how one can succeed doing it.

Chapter 1 is an introduction to overseas schools. Chapter 2 examines the pros and cons of living overseas and working in an international school. Chapter 3 includes a detailed look at a typical international school including the structure, organization, and teachers. Chapters 4 and 5 focus on living and working outside the United States. Chapter 6 previews different regions of the world, including a brief summary of benefits and disadvantages. Chapters 7 through 10 deal with getting a job, interviewing, fairs, and international school organization. Throughout the book I have also asked teachers to add short vignettes about their experiences. Finally, several appendices include a sample resume, cover letter, contract components to look for in your contract, potential interview questions, and the results of the first survey on international teachers using The General Overseas School Survey, TGOSS.

Update in 2016

Since first writing this book four years ago, a lot has changed both personally and professionally. My wife's job has taken us back to the United States and I am actively looking for a job in the DC area and adjusting back to life in the States. After fourteen years visiting the States, there is a different perspective on just about everything. For example, instead of spending the entire summer on the grandparent trail, we are going to visit our families and then take off for a month long trip across the northeast of the United States. For the first time as a couple, we have a choice of where we live and where our children will go to school. This is both exciting and nerve wracking at the same time.

In addition to the changes in my life, a lot of changes have been made to this revised edition. First of all, the book has been edited by a professional writer and editor. He found many mistakes and edits that make this edition more more readable. In addition, he suggested I add more stories of my experiences along the way. Although I did not count, I imagine I added more than than a hundred examples. Another suggestion was to add some tips at the end of each chapter or major section. When appropriate I have added these tips as Extra Credit. Throughout the book I have also asked teachers to add short vignettes about their experiences. Finally, several appendices include a sample resume, cover letter, contract components to look for in your contract, potential interview questions, and the results of the first survey on international teachers using The General Overseas School Survey, TGOSS.

If you have a question, comment, or concern please feel free to reach out to me via email at kentblakeney@gmail.com.

Format of this Book/How to Read

This book can be read from start to finish or by skipping to and from different chapters. If you are a beginning teacher or new to the overseas school experience, you should start at the beginning and read it straight through. Experienced overseas teachers might make use of the chapters dedicated to moving and financial planning. The reference list in the back of the book will lead you to specific topics.

One more note is warranted before continuing. I have taught middle and high school courses equally throughout my career. From these experiences, my perspective leans toward secondary rather than primary teaching. In many chapters you will see this in examples and experiences while in other sections there will be no difference.

In future editions, I hope to expand and include more information pertaining to primary teaching.

How Data was collected

Data for this book comes from a variety of sources, including my personal knowledge of schools. For example, most of Chapter 2 is based on my experiences teaching in six schools and visiting many more around the world. This is somewhat flawed in the sense that these six schools only touch the surface of overseas education. Besides personal knowledge, I also used my experience as a researcher to conduct surveys with teachers, administrators, parents, and students from around the world. This was done through online surveys and personal interviews. I also looked at hundreds of school websites and analyzed what I found. In future editions, I plan to use more research-based techniques to find more data-driven results.

Several books and websites described specific schools, providing demographic information such as enrollment, the number of teachers, leadership structures, and programs offered. There are also a few websites that provide teacher reviews of schools. Chapter 7 contains more information on these resources. If you want specific information on a school, look for that school's website or contact the school. All reputable schools have a well-developed website with information about jobs.

I have tried to present everything from references, but the fact of the matter is many of the insights are mine alone. Meanwhile, one of my aims as an overseas educator and administrator is to collect more data on the art of overseas teaching. At present, this is an area of education that lacks much research. Overseas schools are as diverse as the countries in which they stand. There is no cookie-cutter model. Almost everything I write is this book will not apply to at least a few schools around the world. It's not intended to give you an in-depth look at any one school or region. Instead, I aim to give you an idea of what to expect if you decide to become an overseas teacher.

1 What is An Overseas School?

Broadly defined, an overseas school is a school located outside the United States educating students in English and preparing them for a Western-style university education. 'Overseas' school and 'international' school are interchangeable terms for the purposes of this book. Some overseas schools have established themselves as American schools to emphasize their foundation in the pedagogy of the United States. Many of these schools have names like the International School of _____ or the _____ American School. The name is less important than the structure, organization, nationality of faculty, and educational philosophy. It should be noted that there are international schools in the United States and other English-speaking countries that model themselves as described below and try to find the same students found in overseas schools.

A Quick View of a Typical School

Structure. Although there are many possibilities, the general structure for most overseas schools is similar. Most schools are made up of a parent organization that *owns* the school. The parents vote on a school board, usually five to nine members who vote on broad-reaching items such capital improvements, budgets, hiring of administration, and strategic planning. The board typically oversees a head of school, usually titled the head of school, director or superintendent. Schools are separated into divisions, most often an Elementary School for grades one to five, a Middle School for grades six to eight, and a High School for grades nine to 12. Another common structure is two divisions, usually referred to as Primary (kindergarten and grades one to five) and Secondary (grades six to 12). In any case, each division usually has a principal, and depending on the size, either assistant principals or grade-level coordinators.

Academics/Curriculum. In terms of academics, schools follow a Western curriculum. The vast majority of overseas schools have an individualized curriculum developed by the faculty over time. In recent years many schools have adopted the International Baccalaureate program that consists of a Primary Years Program (grades one to five), Middle Years Program (grades six to 10), and an IB Diploma program (years 11 and 12). Other schools follow more traditional curricula similar to those followed by students in private schools in the United States. Many schools offer Advanced Placement classes for upperclassmen. Still other schools offer combinations of several curricula such as IB and AP classes, and local or national diploma programs. While a U.S. school district has facilities across a city or county, most overseas schools are located on one campus, and some even have everything under one roof. Many, but not all, schools are accredited once every ten years by a regional accrediting authority in the United States. Accreditation should definitely be a consideration when accepting a contract to work at an overseas school.

Teacher Time: Changing Curriculum by Ruth B.

Changing curriculum wasn't something that concerned me too much being a subject specialist. My first overseas post was actually at a local school in New Zealand and not an international school. I was incredibly pleased and surprised to find that the curriculum document was about a fifth of the size of the one I'd used in the UK and left a lot of scope for course content. The curriculum gave targets for skills that must be taught by specific stages and had levels of attainment. The transition wasn't difficult at all and there were always colleagues available for support.

In my first true international school, I found myself teaching the International Baccalaureate Middle Years Program, IB MYP, curriculum and also went through an update of the whole curriculum during this time. The documentation was rather different, as instead of outlining subject-specific skills it focused on approaches to learning. For example, instead of stating that students should be able to perform basic rhythmic patterns, the MYP might ask for students to use knowledge in an abstract setting. In some respects this leaves you with a lot of freedom and every lesson has an element of helping the students develop general learning skills. It did take time to read all of the mark criteria that you had to use and get to grips with the approaches to learning that you needed to incorporate before you could even begin to piece the puzzle together and create a unit. Having said this, it doesn't mean that you can't incorporate fantastic units and resources that you already have. You just have to find a path where you can combine what you have with what you are required to do.

Currently, I teach in a school that uses the British curriculum including the International General Certificate of General Education, IGCSE, program, but instead of A levels we teach IB DP. In all cases there are many resources available online and even courses. The transition this time was smooth as I had previously taught the curriculum, yet I have found myself incorporating ideas from other curriculums that have shaped my teaching.

Regardless of the curriculum you are teaching, your subject knowledge and your teaching style are key to having engaged students.

> *Ruth trained in the UK and teaches whole school Music and Drama. She's been teaching for nearly 10 years and has worked under three different curricula.*

Elementary school. Elementary students will most likely have one teacher and an assistant who are a part of a grade-level team. The schedule might include English, math, science, social studies, special or pull-out activities such as gym, music, art, etc., recess, and a supervised lunch. The student might also have English as a Second Language class, special education, and foreign language classes as needed. After school activities are offered in most schools and typically are run by host country nationals with special skills. In Senegal, the African drumming classes filled up quickly, and even parents took lessons on weekends. As elementary students get older they are more likely to take a second language, have ESL classes if needed, and participate in organized after school activities and sports.

Middle school. Middle schools follow the same pattern as most middle schools in the United States. Students will have the core classes of English, math, science, and social studies. In addition, schools require a second language option, with most students choosing the host country language. French and Spanish are popular options if they are not the host country language. Depending on the schedule, a student would go to four to eight classes a day. In addition, students have a lunch and recess time and possibly an extended advisory, homeroom, or special activity. Depending on their level of English, an ESL student might have anything from a self-contained classroom with several other ESL students to a regular class schedule with some help. More likely than not, ESL students would have something in between such as an ESL class once a day or an ESL teacher helping several students in a regular classroom. After school activities almost always include organized sports teams and academic clubs throughout the year.

High school. High schools are probably the most diverse. In addition to the core subjects of English, math, science, and social studies, students normally accumulate credits over the course of four years with the goal of graduating. Many schools can offer (and are often required to offer) several types of diplomas including an American diploma, a host country diploma, and an International Baccalaureate diploma. Grades nine and ten generally have more structure and fewer choices for students. In many schools, students take IB or AP classes closer to graduation. Depending on the size of the school and the faculty's experience, the number of classes offered can differ greatly. Just like middle school, high school students usually have four to eight classes per day with a lunch and some type of study period, homeroom, or free time. Many educators teach both middle and high school classes. After school, students can participate in a host of clubs, organizations, and sports.

Outside the classroom but still in school. Within the school's confines, you will notice how it is similar to a school in the States. Over time, however, differences will appear. For example, you might realize the school uses A4 rather than A3 paper, there are many staff assistants, and it takes a lot less or a lot more time to get things done. In one school, I am pretty sure the copy machines were older than me, while in Vienna, I had a printer in my room and could print whatever I wanted directly from my computer to the community printers. Your students will most likely be more diverse in terms of first language, ethnicity, background, and international experiences. There is a good chance some of them will come from prominent and wealthy families. Other students will have parents who are diplomats, businesspeople, military officers, or working for non-governmental organizations. Unless you are teaching an upper-level IB or AP class, and even then in some cases, you will have ESL students in your class. Outside the classroom you will notice children speaking languages other than English. Cultural differences might affect all aspects of school including the way you are treated, the foods you eat, and who you interact with on a regular basis. Some parents may contact you constantly while you never meet others. Religious holidays of the host country may make schedules difficult to manage. Students, usually middle and high school more than elementary, may miss many days due to international sporting events, activities, conferences, trips to their home country, college visits and other unforeseen reasons. The school, being independent from regulations, will be more hands off regarding rules and laws. You may be able to do as you wish in the classroom.

Outside school. If you are like most overseas educators, you probably will live in the capital or a large city and relatively close to the school. Instead of a house with a yard, more often than not you will live in an apartment or flat. This varies greatly depending on the school and location. In your first couple of years, you will spend nearly all of your time, including evenings and weekends, around other teachers or people associated with the school. A small percentage of teachers avoid anything related to the school and will not attend any non-mandatory events while others will be at everything.

Your life will be an exciting mix of a somewhat normal school setting and classes followed by a much different life outside school. Even in Western Europe, the differences can be striking. Undoubtedly, you will be treated to some experiences you would not have in the States. If you are living in the developing world, you are presumed to be rich and will be able to afford local luxuries that are within reach of only a handful of the population. Speaking of that, inevitably you will also run into students and parents everywhere from the grocery to bars and restaurants. On breaks, which tend to be quite a bit longer than a typical U.S. school, you might travel with school friends or families to exotic places. Over the summer a good majority of teachers leave the country to travel or head back to their country of origin.

Your contract and finances. Bear in mind that contracts and finances change dramatically from one school to another and what I am describing is a typical school. Most contracts are initially for two years and then renewed in one-, two-, or three-year intervals. Some schools have you sign one-year contracts from the start while others allow for tenure. Most contracts today are structured for all teachers with a standard list of benefits and salary scales. However, some schools write individual contracts based on the school's needs and desirability. There might be some room to negotiate, especially if the position if hard to fill, if the school really needs teachers, or if the candidate has strong skills or experience in a certain area.

Although an individualized contract can be great, it is important to be sure you know what you are signing up for *before* you sign. All administrators in overseas schools are generally happy to discuss details of the contract; be wary of those who are not.

Most contracts include airfare when your contract begins and when it ends. Some pay for the trip back each summer. Schools usually pay for your spouse and children but not pets or other family members. Your base salary will probably be comparable to your salary in the States although this fluctuates greatly depending on the school and its location. Pay scales seem to be the norm and many schools have a cap at which you begin. In my experience, most teachers start with a maximum of around seven years of experience, even if they've been teaching longer. Your kids will usually be enrolled for free although you can expect to pay for extracurricular activities, trips, and other school-related expenses like transportation. Some schools limit the number of children with free tuition but this is often negotiable. This can add up to thousands of dollars a year depending on the number of activities and your location.

Many schools talk about their salaries in terms of what percentage a teacher can save. My experience is that administrators base this on their salaries and general knowledge rather than scientific polling of teacher salaries and benefits. While I am not accusing them of being dishonest, if they are talking to you about this, they probably want you, and will describe the best-case scenario. It also should be noted that your first year will be much more expensive than subsequent years. I once bought a plastic garbage can for the equivalent of $25 when it probably would have cost less than $10 in the States.

Overseas schools also have hugely varied benefits packages. Although there might be great differences between schools in a similar region, there are trends for the different regions of the world. However, elite schools compete for the best teachers, so they will have similar packages regardless of location. Chapter 7 includes more information on regions. A small percentage of schools might pay for a fully furnished house and a car. Some will have an allowance that covers a percentage of your housing. You will almost always be expected to pay a part of the housing as well as other expenses like cable, electricity, water, and trash collection. Still other schools have on-campus living quarters that include everything. Beyond housing, other benefits usually include some form of insurance, a small baggage allowance for the airplane or a weighted shipping allowance. Still other benefits may include access to clubs and commissaries, dental insurance, discounts, mail privileges, and a host of individual school benefits.

Common sense can help a lot when looking at schools. If a school in the middle of a remote country with limited access to the outside world offers you everything above, it might be a sign that it is struggling to hire teachers. If you get the same package from a well-established school in a European capital, it may indicate they can select from hundreds of highly skilled applicants and pick the best of the best.

Most or all of your overseas income will not be taxed in the United States and many countries exempt you from paying local and host country taxes. This can be huge. Using an online reference like the Tax Form Calculator, an income of $57,000 from California will give you the same after-tax income as $42,000 overseas, in addition to all the benefits mentioned in the last few paragraphs.

If you are interested in learning more about investing while overseas, Andrew Hallam has written two books, *Millionaire Teacher* and *The Global Expatriate's Guide to Investing,* and maintains an extensive website at www.andrewhallam.com. It should be noted, Mr. Hallam does not focus on the United States, but has a wealth of good information (get it?)

As far as saving money, it depends on you. It has been my experience that some teachers live extravagant lifestyles, spending their money on luxuries and vacations, saving very little or even going into debt. Parsimonious teaching couples can save more than one person's salary each year and have a huge amount of savings after just a few years. A lot of this depends on your location and the school. Naturally, some cities are much more expensive than others. You and your family will likely be somewhere in the middle. Depending on your lifestyle, you will be able to save a moderate amount of your income while living a moderate lifestyle. Unfortunately, to get into overseas education, you might spend the first years getting your feet in the door and not saving much. Getting my foot in the door meant beginning as a "local hire" with no benefits. I spent more than I earned the first year but more than doubled my income with a nice benefits package at my second overseas school.

Final thoughts. Hopefully you have a much better idea of what teaching overseas is like. While you might not follow a path exactly as I have described, it will at least be similar. Some people find that teaching overseas was the best idea they ever had and find themselves professionally and financially satisfied. A small percentage find they were duped by the person who recruited them, have a horrible experience, and break their contract before the end of the first year. Some teachers spend their whole career in one school and assimilate into the host country. Most schools cap the number of years you can stay (usually 10), after which your benefits may be reduced or contract not renewed.

One of the greatest benefits of teaching overseas is the freedom it offers. Having relatively short contracts, it is not uncommon to stay in one school a few years and then move on to the next school. For most career overseas teachers, five-to-seven years in one place is the norm. Traveling in different parts of the world can be a mixture of excitement and frustration, but above all, more memorable than the life you leave behind. Many teachers often talk about how they left the States twenty or thirty years ago and haven't looked back.

Having traveled extensively around the world before and after deciding to live overseas, one thing I am sure of is that working overseas has provided me with many opportunities both on and off the typical tourist track. The relationships I have formed with teachers, parents, and host country nationals have been rewarding and fulfilling.

Extra Credit: To learn more about a school, you can find a lot online. If you have an offer from a school, you can ask to email a few teachers. You could also do this yourself; many schools post faculty bios and email addresses on their websites. A few sites *review* overseas schools; however, many of the reviews are skewed by disgruntled former employees. I've read the reviews of every overseas schools I worked at and concluded that most of these reviews should be taken with a grain of salt.

2 Pros and cons of living and working in an overseas School

same time it can be expensive, lonely, and frustrating. I've spent days on my motorcycle traveling through remote areas of Nepal while I've also spent two hours in a bank line only to find out that I had to come back the next day due to a power outage. A list of pros and cons is obviously going to be different for everyone. One person may hate the food in a country while someone else thinks it is the best they've ever tasted.

This is an attempt to put together some of the 'truths.' It is by no means complete and there is certainly room for debate. The purpose of this chapter is to give you an idea of what overseas teachers think.

At School

Pros

Work with experienced faculty who hold many of the same values as you: In every school there is bound to be a group of teachers that have similar interests as you. If not, you need to adapt. In the last year, I switched from being an avid racquetball player who thought squash was for Europeans to an avid squash player who is flabbergasted there are only four squash courts in my home state of Kentucky.

Save a portion of your salary: Even in the most expensive markets in the world, there are ways to make money through tutoring, renting your apartment while you're away over the summer break, and selling plasma. A friend of mine doubled his take home salary by teaching two SAT prep courses when he lived in London.

No central office or state-mandated standards: You usually have much more freedom to do what you want, when you want, how you want, as long as the kids are learning. One of my colleagues spent a few weeks after the AP exams having students put together an impressive Rube Goldberg apparatus in his classroom.

Administration is more willing to allow you to innovative: If you can make a reasonable argument, chances are your school will let you do it.

Smaller classes: While my thoughts have changed over the years about smaller classes, the largest I've had overseas is twenty-four students; most are between fifteen to twenty students. I once taught a Model United Nations class that started with ten students and ended with nine different students. Only one stayed the whole year.

Access to technology: One thing separating overseas schools from local schools is the access to technology. More and more schools are going to one-to-one laptop program in secondary and lots of access to technology in primary grades.

Sense of community is strong: While living in a fishbowl can have its drawbacks, being a teacher at an overseas school can feel a lot like freshman year of college. You start in a big group with people doing everything together but eventually break into small groups. In small and medium schools, functions like BBQs and parties are usually invite-all affairs. I've noticed that the larger the school, the smaller the circle of friends one typically has.

Diverse student body: Most true international schools have students from literally around the world. My dad was amazed when he went to one of my classes last year. Having never seen me teach, I thought he might mention how good a job I did. No, he mentioned how diverse the students were. We went on to discover that the ten students came from eight different countries and spoke as many different native languages. That is just one way students are diverse. You might also find one student goes wherever he wants on the weekend in the family jet while another in the same class shares his bedroom with two siblings.

No union fees to pay: Leaving politics aside, not paying union fees is a good feeling. Some schools have teacher associations with minimal dues but you are likely to pay more to your sunshine committee. At the same time, some schools do not renew contracts or ask teachers to leave.

Cons

May not have a curriculum or resources needed to teach effectively: With so much turnover coupled by lots of freedom, curriculum usually takes a back seat to instruction until it comes times for the ever-dreaded accreditation visit.

Limited special needs program: Many schools accept students with special needs in spite of the fact that most educators have very little professional development or experience with special needs students. While most schools will not allow absolutely every student in, it is hard to turn anyone down if there is space available.

Students may not be academically qualified: Being able to pay the fees may supersede academic prowess. It is no surprise that many schools are focusing on differentiation for professional development.

Parents can be very direct and do not understand the Western style of education: Some students have parents with powerful jobs. You might be expected to do something you do not feel comfortable doing but would be expected in the host country culture. It is not easy telling a former prime minister that his son isn't getting an A. In a few instances, such as teaching a royal family or president's child, you may have to put your hands in the air and hope you don't get "PNG'd" (persona non grata).

Overbearing administration or board and no outlet to share grievances: There is not too much you can do if you feel your administration or board is treating you unfairly. If it is really bad, you can either break contract and leave or suck it up until your contract expires. While this is relatively rare, it happens enough that it is worth mentioning.

Administration may be reluctant to enforce certain rules or policies: From my experience, you can expect some help from your administrators for major issues like drugs on campus; however, don't expect them to do much when it comes to minor offenses like absences, tardiness, and disrespect. I am not sure why, but these problems are not top priorities for many administrators.

Expensive job fairs: Jobs fairs are usually held in big cities like Bangkok, London, and Boston. If you live in the States you can expect to spend at least $1,000 for a three-day job fair and probably a bit more. If you are already overseas, it might wipe out your savings. While the pendulum swung towards hiring by Skype a few years ago, it seems like it might be swinging back toward job fairs at the moment.

May share a classroom: As schools expand, there is a period of few years when classes are full and space is limited. Don't be surprised if you are expected to share your classroom in some capacity. This might be a class, an advisory or homeroom, or an after-school activity. I had to hide my whiteboard markers and erasers at one school as about 2,000 students came to the campus on Saturdays to learn English and had a reputation for taking everything that wasn't bolted to the ground.

Poor facilities: Surprisingly, some schools have some pretty shitty facilities. I've often thought that if I were spending $20,000 a year per child, I'd expect a much more than this.

Grade Inflation: Many different stakeholders expect grades to be good for students. This could mean an email from a parent asking if a child can redo an assignment. I have had students email or ask in person if I can just change a grade. At the same time, schools like to display where there students have been accepted to university.

No union to protect your interests: As mentioned before, in many places, you do not have options if you feel you are being treated unfairly. My best advice would be to ask an experienced, well-liked teacher to help. The U.S. consulate or your embassy may help if you are in a real pickle and need to get out of the country in a hurry. While not exactly related, the only time overseas I did not have access to my passport (because the school was getting a resident visa), I was picked up by the police at a bar. They were looking for a gringo fugitive. After getting a ride to the station in the back of a police truck with a friend and six policemen, I called the U.S. Embassy duty officer. They let us go before putting us in jail.

Living Overseas

Pros

Access to a new culture, language, religion, and set of values: If you have decided to move overseas, you will inevitably have to adjust to differences between your culture and the one you come from. This holds true as well when you move from one place to another. My experience has been that I generally find these cultural differences to be "wrong" until I assimilate into the country. For example, I do not think that I would ever buy a motorcycle in the

States but I have bought motorcycles in three of the countries I have lived in. Before your eyebrows go much higher, let me explain. In many other countries, there are a lot more motorcycles so people are accustomed to motorcycles and how to drive around motorcycles. At least for now you also don't have to worry about people texting, eating, shaving their legs, or anything like that when driving. In other words, people tend to be more aware.

Travel regionally, nationally, or internationally: Rather than spending a weekend going to big box stores and fast food restaurants, living overseas avails you the opportunity to discover the area around you on a regular basis. For example, going to the market may end up being a regular occurrence to see what new items have come in and find out more about the culture. In most countries, it would take years of weekends and long weekends to travel to all the tourist places within a country. Wanting more, most countries have great regional travel opportunities that are a short drive or plane flight away. Think about it, you will be able to do a weekend trip that people from the States would consider a trip of a lifetime. Not having to get over jet lag and knowing a little about the culture and language can be very helpful as well.

Cultural awareness: Living in a country and understanding it can go a long way. By understanding the culture you can dig way deeper into a country than the average tourist. It is amazing how many teachers end up with close local friends, hang out at restaurants and bars that are off the beaten path but still "gems", and volunteer with local organizations.

Meeting interesting like-minded people: Not everyone would consider moving to another country to teach. Right there, you and all the other teachers (and parents) in the community will have a common connection. I have never been to a school where any teacher did not find at least a few other teachers that they became friends with. Unlike many schools in the States, you will probably see you colleagues outside of school a lot. While there are a few teachers that stick to themselves by choice, most are very agreeable to hanging out after work.

Self-realization: There are many things that I have learned about myself by living overseas. The biggest one for me is my ability to be patient when I need to. In fact, this year my New Year's Resolution was "F*&$ It" when I encountered a problem that I thought could be easily be handled. You'd be surprised how many times I said that in my head in the last year. Regardless of how long you live overseas, you will definitely learn a lot about yourself.

Extra Credit: If you are expecting a lot of visitors, you might want to wait on some of the local or regional tourist opportunities until you have guests. Also, if you have a local identification or residency card, ask for the local rate. It can be quite a bit cheaper. One more tidbit, you can also probably find someone at school to buy tickets for certain things for a nominal fee. For example, in Senegal, you can wait hours to get a ferry ticket. Local staff at the school had spouses who were willing to go down and wait in the line for me and they were happy to do it. They were also happy to get a ten dollars for the effort, which was the equivalent of a few days food.

Cons

Distance from other cities and people: Some schools are very isolated from other cities. You may be at a school in a regional capital and long for a school in a more cosmopolitan city or at least one with a McDonalds.

Limited access to Western food products, and media: If there is anything you can't live without, you should bring it. While many big cities have just about everything you need, the items may be somewhat different or very expensive. Some might even have more; however, you are most likely not going to see many big box stores in many parts of the world. Imports are often ridiculously priced as well. You'll probably have to adapt some of your food choices. I quit eating chicken in Africa because I just didn't like the taste. Getting media is usually not much of an issue if you use a VPN or decide to use other less scrupulous methods. However, it is getting a bit more difficult. We had Netflix overseas and then all of the sudden it quit working because Netflix started using a geo locator to find us. This part of your life can be really frustrating and pervasive.

Difficulty in a medical crisis: While many people complain about health care in the U.S., it can get much worse. It is important to learn where the best medical facility in your community is in the first few weeks (or even days). Taking a dry run to physically identify it would be a wise idea. Its also a good idea to bring as much medicine as you think you might need when first moving to a country. Almost all schools have nurses that can be very helpful. As well, the Embassy may be able to help through their American Services in dire cases. It also might worth checking out medivac insurance for really bad problems and finding out what your school offers with their insurance package.

Hard for individuals, especially females, in some locations: Unfortunately some places are not as tolerant of expatriates as others. In remote locations it can be really difficult if the community is weary of expatriates or has had trouble with past expatriates. In some countries women are not treated well, especially expatriates. In Nepal, I heard that women have a lower standing than men, boys, and even animals. In Nicaragua, it was impossible to walk down the street without getting catcalls. This can work both ways. One of my Nicaraguan friends came back from her first year of college in States and found her self-esteem had dropped because men in the States were *not* whistling or giving her catcalls. While catcalls or outright disrespect has never been an issue for me, I have been in many conversations where this was the subject. Not knowing the local language sometimes can be helpful as you won't know what people are saying about you.

Access to watching sports and live TV: As an avid sports fan, it has been difficult to keep up with teams and sports in the States. This was most difficult in Nepal where we were 11:45 ahead of the East coast. It is better in Europe and Africa with a time difference of about four to seven hours. Central and South America are not a problem regarding time. If the time is not the problem, it may be difficult to actually get the game. However, other locations might be easy. In Nicaragua, the regular cable service included all four major networks and ESP, all in English. I have been lucky to have the Armed Forces Network through the US Embassy. I also bought the NFL package to watch my favorite team. In a nutshell, if you really really really want to watch a game, you can probably make it happen most of the time. I don't think I've missed a NFL game of my favorite team in about five or six years. If sports are not your thing but you like watching live events this will be an issue. It is not surprising to hear someone walk up to the lunch table and say, "Please don't tell me about the Oscars, I'm watching them after school" or "if you know the score of the game please don't tell me." If you are interested, a few options include slingTV, slingbox, and purchasing sports leagues overseas packages if they are offered. Go Steelers!

Limited ability to express yourself as you might in the U.S.: Since moving overseas, I have had to become much more guarded in what I say and how I express my personal beliefs. This has not been a major issue for me and it's something I can accept as part of living overseas; however, it can be very difficult. Here are a few examples. In one country a teacher was asked to leave or resigned after creating a podcast that included some controversial subjects including some that related directly to the school. Sometimes people that are LGBTQ+ need to be very discreet as local laws or customs may strictly forbid it. Dating locals can also be quite difficult in some countries. I heard of a Peace Corps volunteer getting kicked out of Morocco for kissing his local girlfriend in public. As a general rules of thumb, if you think something might get you in trouble, you might want to refrain saying or doing it. Talking about the local government, especially in class, can be extremely foolish. Many schools around the world have children of presidents, prime ministers, and royalty. Keep in mind that you are really of guest of the government that has much more power than you or the school when discussing sensitive topics.

Loneliness, especially during holidays: Loneliness can be a real downer while living overseas. This was my biggest personal issue before joining the Peace Corps. I didn't know if I could handle being by myself so much. Now, I really enjoy time by myself and regularly eat and even go to movies by myself. I would have never done that before moving overseas. Holidays, especially that first year can be really difficult. Luckily, the Internet helps a lot. There will inevitably be people that get together for holidays as well. Many school heads will also host events for first year teachers for Thanksgiving. All of the schools I have taught in have had some type of Holiday party in December.

Extra Credit: Always take the maximum amount of bags when leaving your country of residence so that you can bring stuff back. It is pretty amazing how much food one can fit in a second piece of luggage. People have even bought coolers, filled them with meat, then sold the cooler to another expat when returning to their country of residence. Another idea is to bring spices when you first move somewhere. They are small, can easily fit in a suitcase and can make a big difference.

Difficulties Teaching Overseas by Unoma A.

International teaching is made all the more interesting because apart from dealing with the regular issues of the job like tons of marking, assessments, planning, extra-curricular activities, management decisions, etc., an international teacher has to settle into a new lifestyle in a new country with its own peculiar customs and traditions. He/she has to be careful in seemingly regular daily interactions, as a seemingly simple statement that has been misunderstood can cause a multitude of problems. For example, when I was in Egypt a child complained that his classmate had called him "'inta gazma" which means a shoe. I laughed because I found it funny that someone would get so upset about being called a shoe but the child was really upset. His parents got involved even though I had told the offender to apologize. In a foreign place, with no family or friends to comfort you, at such times, international teaching can create feelings of intense loneliness.

Another downside to international teaching is trying to implement the curriculum correctly. Parents are not cooperative and have their own agenda that they want the school to follow especially if they are influential members of the society. Parents of 3- and 4-year-olds expect their little ones to be able to read through a dictionary and write epistles at this age and thus make it difficult to focus more on social and emotional development to get the child psychologically prepared for life outside the home environment that they have been used to for so long.

Having no sense of a place to call home is another aspect of international teaching that can be quite disconcerting. Moving from country to country or school to school can be exasperating and the hassles of work permits and visas can be stressful. Making friends and having to move away and leave them soon afterwards can also be quite emotionally dissatisfying. Social media helps but it's not the same as hanging out face to face.

In addition, living away from home for too long can make you feel alienated from your country, family and friends. You start questioning values and practices you never considered as unnecessary before embarking on an international teaching career.

Unoma A. is currently working on her Master's in Special Education and has taught in Nigeria, Egypt, The United Kingdom, and Tanzania.

3 The School

The purpose of this chapter is to give you a more personal look at what to expect from an overseas school. It will look at the structure and organization, facilities, curriculum, administration, special education and politics, both in and out of school. A second part will compare differences in schools based on the number of students. The chapter finishes with a look at different types of schools including public and private, Department of Defense schools, and Department of State supported schools. Let's get started.

Structure and Organization

The school board. Schools come in a variety of shapes and sizes, but the majority are organized with a school board comprised of parents who were elected by parents of active students. Boards typically have five to ten members, including a board president, vice president, secretary, and treasurer. Sometimes, boards require certain nationalities to be represented. For example, a school might require at least a majority of the board be from the United States. As per usual board governance, they often have committees, hold regular structured meetings (usually once per month), and have both open and closed sessions. There is usually a time during open session for teachers, parents, and even students to ask questions or raise concerns.

Your role with the board might vary greatly depending on the school. In some schools, the teachers are a part of the association that votes for the board. In effect, this allows the teachers to vote in a large bloc to elect board members the teachers think will serve their needs. In other schools, you may not be part of the association and have no voting rights. While this is probably not a make-or-break part of a contract, having a vote or at least representation on the board is almost always positive. Most teachers, especially new ones, will have little or no communication with their school's board. However, it is likely that one of the board members will be the parent of one of your students.

As far as the legalities of overseas schools, laws differ from country to country. Many schools were founded by a charter or law that established the school and gave them certain exclusive rights not normally found in public or private schools in the country. Many include clauses such as tax exemptions and not-for-profit status. Other schools might have been formed in other manners such as word-of-mouth or handshake agreements through an individual and someone in the government. In recent years, the number of for-profit, proprietary schools seems to have increased dramatically. According to the International School Consultancy Group, there are over 7,000 schools with 3.5 million students in English-medium schools. Much of this growth has been seen in Asia and the Middle East.

Extra Credit:

Even if you are not required to attend a school board meeting, you should go to one just to see what happens and have some context in case you are ever asked to make a presentation, or must attend for other reason.

The head of school. Just below the school board is the head of school. For perspective, this person is somewhat like a superintendent in the United States. Some schools have other terms for this position such as superintendent, director, or president, but they all essentially cover the same areas. The director may have hired you or been a factor in the hiring process. Almost surely they will send you a congratulatory email or phone call upon being hired. Beyond this, unless you are on a committee or the school is quite small, the director will probably not be a part of your daily life. In fact, in many schools the director's office and staff are located in separate buildings or away from academic classrooms. In some really large schools, the office may not even be on the same campus.

The director's responsibilities are important for the school to remain successful and move forward. Directors spend their days talking to the school's business manager, administrators, and board members. A typical week might include a meeting with the regional security officer of the U.S. Embassy to discuss campus security, a discussion with the head of a mining operation that is considering pulling out of the country and taking twenty students, a cocktail party with ministers and ambassadors, an elementary play, meeting with the architect and lawyers about buying new property, and evaluating you.

Their duties are to make sure the school is well run, achieving its mission, and moving forward in a positive direction. As such, a director might spend a lot of time working on the budget and strategic plan. On a side note, don't be surprised when you are asked during your first few months about what supplies you need for next year. Most schools buy supplies from the States and it can take close to year to actually get them to the school. Although they might wander the halls occasionally, most directors have graduated from daily contact with students and spend their time running the school as a business or organization. One of their most important duties is supervising the school's divisional principals.

Typically, each school has a principal in each division. In small schools the principal might also be the director or even teach a few classes. Most principals come from the United States, have a lot of experience in overseas education, served as a teacher, and have postgraduate degrees. However, there are certainly principals who have none or just one of these qualities. Each school and director is different in what they want and need regarding this tier of leadership.

Principals have almost all the same responsibilities as those in the United States. They oversee a group of teachers and students in certain grade levels, hold meetings, evaluate teachers, drive the curriculum, meet with parents, make sure report cards go out on time, etc. Unlike many principals in the States, overseas principals do not spend an inordinate amount of time doing bureaucratic paperwork. For example, as schools generally have a small or nonexistent special education program, most principals do not spend their time in Individualized Education Plan meetings.

One of the biggest differences in many schools is the level of autonomy for principals and teachers. Many overseas schools are exempt from most or all education laws within the country. As mentioned before, most schools do have some requirements such as offering a host country's diploma or a U.S. diploma, but the requirements generally tend to be more lax.

Assistant principals and grade-level coordinators tend to be at larger schools as the need arises. Their role is to support the teachers and principals. As the needs of a school change, so do the job descriptions of the assistant principals. In some schools, they will focus on discipline, while at others they might work more with teachers and curriculum.

The rest of the staff. If you have never worked in a really small community or an independent private school, the amount of periphery staff might be surprising. Not only are overseas schools like little districts under one roof, they are in different countries which often requires special staff. For example, many schools have someone on staff dedicated to new students.

The front office or director's office is often full of competent host country nationals and a few overseas managers. However, in certain countries, the front office could be made up of all host country nationals. The front office usually includes a business manager/finance person, admissions office, and a secretary/receptionist. In large schools this could be a team of several dozen people working in several offices and buildings. Some other common positions are a director's assistant, receptionist, alumni officer, and human resources director.

Other important staff members outside the director's office include divisional administrative assistants, IT department, cafeteria staff, and maintenance staff. For the most part, these staff members are combination of host country nationals with varying abilities of English and a few overseas staff in leadership positions.

Extra Credit: It is important to be on good terms with the person in charge of maintenance (especially if they are in charge your house, too), the best IT person, and the administrative assistant in your division. Make a point to meet each of them and know their names above all others. This might come in handy when your house floods on Saturday night, you forgot to print out a set of tests, or you need a sub next block.

Curriculum

Curriculum is a touchy subject in overseas schools for several reasons. It goes without saying that developing, implementing, and revising a curriculum requires a great deal of skill and time for teachers, administrators, and everyone else. For this reason, many districts in the United States are given a curriculum or at least a framework, like the Common Core Standards. Remember that many teachers sign relatively short contracts, so there is little incentive to write a curriculum. It is time consuming from a whole school and individual classroom approach, and many believe it is restrictive. I have also noticed that some administrators do not put curriculum at the top of their priority lists.

The idea of a curriculum in overseas schools has changed greatly over the past several years. Although I have seen schools with little or no curriculum, schools with a broad scope and sequence, and schools with a fully developed curriculum, it is clear that *if* schools seek accreditation from a regional association from the United States, they will need to have a curriculum. This might not have been the case in past accreditation visits.

Curricula in overseas schools are difficult to develop. Not only must a school create a curriculum that allows students to graduate with an IB diploma, AP classes, and a national diploma, but it also must incorporate the host country language, other languages, an ESL program, technology, special needs program, and non-core classes. Keep in mind that a typical school will have many non-native English-speaking teachers and things get sticky quickly.

Schools that are considered IB World schools follow the IB program from the early years through graduation. This obviously has some positive and negative aspects. It appears the early years program (years one to five) and graduate program (years 11 and 12) have a much stronger reputation than the middle years program (years six through 10). Adopting the IB program is expensive compared to other options. Many schools opt for the IB graduate program rather than the early and middle years programs. In such cases, schools might use a backward-by-design model at least through the middle school to prepare students for the IB graduate program.

Most other curriculum models in overseas schools tend to follow similar models to the United States. For example, a student might be required to have three or four full years of core classes and a sliding scale of other classes depending on other graduation requirements.

Elementary curricula are typically developed out of scope and sequences developed by individual teachers in the school. This may be highly developed using the latest resources and best practices or at the whim of the teacher.

The curricula in many schools have likely developed over time and are very fluid. In my experience in six schools on four continents, the curricula in five of the six schools have been inadequate. For example, one of my classes was not even listed in the curriculum materials when I arrived at the school even though it had been taught for years. Do not be surprised to find yourself in a school where curriculum only comes up every five or ten years (before an accreditation visit). I have personally seen thematic units taught three times in three years and other important subjects like the history of the local country not covered at all.

The Office of Overseas Schools from the U.S. Department of State has developed a set of standards called the Aero Standards. This includes access to workshops, resources, and consultations. It seems the focus is on math and science, but there are resources for English/language arts, social studies, music, visual arts, and world languages. Much more information can be found online, at projectaero.org.

Extra Credit: If you have experience writing curriculum be sure to let your future administrator know this to stand out over other candidates, and especially if you want to develop and improve your skills in curriculum development. Many schools use a counselor, assistant principal, head librarian, or someone with many other job descriptions to lead curriculum development. If there are any black holes or dark spots in overseas education, curriculum is one of them.

Exceptional Learners

Exceptional learners fall into three categories: children with the academic ability to achieve more than their peers, those with a learning disability precluding them from performing at the same level as their peers without some type of assistance, and students who do not have a full grasp of English. You will undoubtedly encounter all in any overseas school. It is important to remember that almost all schools receive the vast amount of their operating costs from tuition fees. As well, many families move to a country with an exceptional student and have limited or no options other than your school because of language requirements and their past overseas experience. Moreover, the administration usually decides who is and is not accepted. While a small minority of schools accepts any student, almost all overseas schools are somewhat selective. A student who may be borderline but able to pay the full tuition is likely to be in your classes. In reality, each student represents a certain amount of tuition money available to support the school.

Most students who might be considered *gifted and talented* in the United States usually take a normal load of classes with some exceptions for higher-level learning. Students with other exceptionalities such as ADHD, ADD, and learning disabilities may have support from a teacher with a background in special education. Students with more severe learning disabilities such as blindness will need an added level of support not typically accessible in overseas schools. The next few sections will cover students in each of these groups.

One of the benefits of overseas schools is teaching students who are exceptionally talented in one or more areas. Considering that the vast majority of host country national and expatriate students have parents who are successful, driven, and educated, the percentage of highly achieving students might surprise you. As well, you might find students who are high achieving and willing to do whatever it takes to succeed because of cultural expectations.

The nature of many overseas schools dictates that with the drive, resources, training, and talent, a great teacher generally has more freedom with students. Differentiation and other methods can allow these students to excel beyond the limits of the regular classroom at all levels. For example, a first-grade student with an exceptional ability in math could be allowed to work with a math specialist rather than the regular first grade math. As the student progresses, he or she can be put in advanced classes or independent studies without much difficulty. Advanced classes can be offered at a younger age than normal. It is not uncommon to have a small percentage of middle school students taking an advanced math or language class with high school students. Schools typically structure schedules to accommodate these learners.

With that being said, it is unfortunate that many schools do not have the resources or structure to accommodate all highly achieving students. For example, a small school may only have a few options for advanced-level social studies classes. In these cases, differentiation or independent studies are the norm. Although these are somewhat effective, it is clear from my experience that larger schools or those with more resources typically have more options for highly achieving students. As a first-year teacher in six different schools, I have noticed that I am doing well if I just get through the curriculum. Sometimes certain aspects of teaching that I would love to accomplish have been put to the wayside to ensure that all students are at least learning the core content.

Motivation can also be a factor. One example comes to mind. A student of mine a few years ago was immensely gifted in social studies, specifically a class I taught in preparation for a Model United Nations trip to Dublin, Ireland. It was like pulling teeth to get this student to do much of anything in class although I knew he had a worldview and understanding that far surpassed other students in his grade. When it came time to defend his country at the conference, he gave a two-minute speech to 800 peers. They gave him a standing ovation; the only one I've ever seen at a Model UN Conference. He won the highest award: Most Distinguished Speaker. To this day, I still cannot figure out why I could not get that same passion out of him in class. I wish I could have harnessed that type of motivation in him all year.

In a more typical situation among high-performing kids, a student or two in each class will do what is minimally required to receive a decent grade. At a minimum, you should have some type of differentiation for these students, extended activities, challenge problems when they complete the normal classroom requirements. Differentiation for these students should extend rather than reinforce regular classroom content and activities. This is something that an administrator might ask during an interview to gauge your teaching ability.

There are many other exceptional students in overseas schools. There are students with ADHD, ADD, and a host of other diagnoses. These students are typically given accommodations that allow them to complete the work in the curriculum. For example, a student with processing difficulties might be given an accommodation on tests that allows him to set up an essay problem using a graphic organizer. Many students are given extra time on assessments. Schools will generally accept these students if they are able to take regular classes and do not need so many accommodations that the schools take on more than they can handle. In reality, this sometimes happens and students who probably are not best suited for your overseas school will be in your class. If no other options are available, you will be asked to do your best to serve the student and the others in the classroom. This can lead to some complicated decisions on how to best manage your time, both in the classroom and planning.

Students with severe disabilities are usually turned away because overseas schools don't have the infrastructure, training, and resources to satisfy the needs of the students. A few schools around the world might make exceptions for students on an individual basis. For example, a deaf student who has a full-time assistant provided by the family might be accepted. Governments might provide resources for certain students with severe disabilities. I have heard of only a handful of students with severe disabilities. Many overseas teachers probably go their entire career overseas without being in a school with severely disabled student.

English as a Second Language

Almost every overseas school has an English as Second Language program. ESL classes generally follow the same format from school to school although there are several models from which to follow. Many schools limit the percentage of non-native English speakers in each regular class although other schools may have near 100 percent of the students as English language learners. Depending on the level of need, most students might have pullout ESL classes for a few months to a few years followed by an inclusion program. This might also be supported by special classes for writing and reading. Here is a little more detail about each division.

Elementary ESL students can be divided into two groups: grade two and younger, and grades three through five. The students from grades two and below are typically placed in a regular English-speaking classroom. The student might have extra help from a classroom aide. It is amazing to see how much a 6-year-old can learn in a year. As this model seems to work universally, it is most likely the method at your school. The older elementary grades might use the same model as younger grades, add some support such as a pullout English class, or provide a more structured English language program. As students move to middle school and high school, English becomes harder to teach and students take longer to learn it.

Many middle school and early high school models provide specialized ESL teachers whose sole responsibility is to teach a small group of students English in a short period of time. The model I have seen most often is an intensive pullout ESL model for all core classes. Students learn English, science, and language arts in the ESL classroom with a small group of students. Math is dependent on the student's ability and the school's policy. Students go to other classes such as physical education, music, art, computers, etc. with their peers in their class. As students qualify, they are moved into an inclusion model where the ESL teacher goes to the regular classroom to help the student. This might be one class or all of them. Another method is an additional class in which the students have extra support in writing, reading, and speech. As students get older, English becomes more important, especially when taking IB or AP classes. As such, many schools require a certain level of proficiency for students to enter in high school or even late middle school.

Schools use what works and what is effective. Factors that may affect an ESL program are teacher resources, class schedules, the number of students in the ESL program, and the level of interest and training by regular classroom teachers. I have seen ESL teachers who are highly qualified and trained to teach ESL students, teachers asked to take an extra block to fulfill contractual requirements, and parents asked to step in at the last minute. Some schools do not seem to place a great amount of emphasis on the quality of ESL teacher while other schools realize its importance.

There are several portals on the Internet that provide ESL training online.

Extra Credit: If you have an opportunity, do some professional development with a focus on ESL. This might be advantageous for you as a new teacher. It shows you are serious about working overseas and there will always be a certain number of ESL students or recent ESL students in your classes. More importantly, you will have some knowledge of ESL pedagogy that will help ESL students in your classroom.

School Politics

Overseas schools can be more political than schools in the States. The board is often made up of parents who had solid reasons for wanting to be on the board. In all likelihood, they want to make some type of change. Parents not on the board often have high positions such as ambassadors, CEOs of corporations, ministers, and high-ranking military officers. They are not accustomed to going up the chain-of command to get answers; they go straight to the top. Other influential groups include teachers, the administration, parents who stay at home, and everyone in between.

Politics usually boil down to being government-related (host country government, your government, or another government) or school-related. Be especially careful when talking publicly about the host country. Some countries have laws against certain actions or speech. Something you say in class could possibly get you thrown out of the country as persona non grata. You should not be timid about teaching, but be careful. For example, if one speaks poorly of the king in a country that has a ruling monarchy, it is possible one of the students will report back to their parents. The parents might report it to a high-ranking government official. This could get ugly quickly. It is best to leave these kinds of issues alone. Although this did not happen at the school, one of my friends in one of the countries I taught in left the country rapidly after an internal report containing politically sensitive information was leaked from the office she worked in.

School politics are a different ballgame. From my experience, school politics usually revolve around an administrator or teacher that a group of parents do not like or it's a religious issue. Some parents run for the board, or create an ad-hoc group that meets regularly to discuss the faults of an administrator or teacher. Although sometimes the criticisms might be pertinent, the method is not. Parents, like all stakeholders, should go through proper channels to raise grievances against administrators or teachers. Unfortunately they do not. If this is happening to you, try to get ahead of it by working with your divisional principal or school head. Having solid information, facts, and data to support your methods and teaching can go a long way to diffuse potential situations. Religious issues come up often. Different religious sects want certain holidays off or events (such as dances) canceled. In my experience, the comments are noted but little is done.

Intra-school politics is another issue altogether. Just like every organization with a large group of employees, some people do not get along. Occasionally this is an administrator who is disliked by the staff or an administrator who dislikes a teacher or group of teachers. Steer clear! Provide guidance and a listening ear at your own peril. Sometimes experienced teachers vie for the friendship of new teachers in an attempt to create allies. Sometimes teammates or teachers in the same grade do not get along.

When dealing with the politics at school it is best to let others get involved if they want; you should be an observer. When confronted by a parent or board member about something, it might be best to deflect the question to your principal and note that you do not have enough information to give the person a good answer. You could also tell them you will get back to them later, once you have more information.

Almost all schools have a person who represents the faculty to the board. If you feel strongly enough, talk to that person about the problem and ask them to move it up the chain of command without using your name. In any case, do not get yourself in trouble by answering a question or making a comment without giving time for reflection and guidance.

Extra Credit: Unless you have a conflict mediation license, try not to get yourself involved unless it is directly affecting your work or teaching. If it goes wrong, there are not many places to hide in an overseas school. As a last resort, get the administration involved or ask to move to another team or part of the school.

School Size

Schools come in many different sizes and shapes. Much of this depends on what is available in the country. Major factors influencing school size are the number of host country nationals willing to pay for the school, the number of overseas families, the political situation, and alternative school choices.

Small schools (5-100 students) Small schools usually exist to give a small number of students an English-language education in an area that otherwise would have nothing to offer. For example, an oil company might create a school for a group of twenty English-speaking students. A few years back, I attended the Association of Independent Schools of Africa conference with the entire staff of a school, all five teachers and one administrator. The International School of Belize had an enrollment of twenty-two in 2016. Another small school might be located on a Pacific island that has a small, poverty-stricken population that cannot afford to attend an overseas school. More than likely an international corporation or a for-profit will own the school. The administration and number of teachers will probably be much smaller and often more diverse than larger schools. These schools are not very common and living in such remote areas can be considerably more difficult. However, almost all schools start with small numbers and grow with the oldest group of students.

Medium-sized schools (100-350 students) Medium-sized schools are much more common than small schools. They are scattered throughout the world in smaller cities in developed countries and many capital cities of developing countries, like the American School of Lesotho, which has 169 students, more than half of which are in elementary school. The structure, ownership, and administration of these schools are much more likely to be similar to typical overseas schools, just on a smaller scale. For example, the school building might be purpose-built for education but instead of having three divisions the school may be divided into two. There may be fewer administrators and the director might also be a divisional principal. Teachers often have four or five different classes to teach (especially in the middle and high school).

Working in a medium-sized school has advantages and disadvantages. Benefits include access to some or many modern comforts, more expat socialization, advancement possibilities, and more opportunities outside the school. Disadvantages to consider are the location, safety, access to transportation, activities outside work hours, and feeling more like you are living in fishbowl.

Large schools (350-800 students) Most large schools are in the developed world or very large urban centers in the developing world. These schools will be large enough that a teacher will not know the names of all the employees at the school. The American International School of Vienna has several gyms, libraries, and divisions with about 800 students and over 100 teachers. The structure, ownership, and administration would be similar to the picture of an overseas school described earlier in the chapter. Students intermingle less between grades, and teachers in the secondary division are more likely to teach fewer different courses.

There are many advantages and a few disadvantages of working at a large school. Advantages include more on-campus resources, such as computer labs, bigger libraries, more assistants, and fewer courses (preps) for each teacher. In most schools, you could live in an area of town without seeing students outside of school; the fishbowl is now a swimming pool. Disadvantages include the anonymity of working in an organization with many employees, teaching only one class, getting lost in the shuffle, and living in an environment in which the teachers do not mingle very much outside of school.

Extra-large schools (800-3,500 students) The largest overseas schools are almost always located in huge population centers. Many of these schools have multiple campuses, though few have more than 1,500 students on one campus. As might be expected at a school this large, there are people dedicated to just about every activity on campus, resources are plentiful, and there is a huge range of activities and clubs for students. The Shanghai American School has over 3,000 students and more than 400 teachers in two separate campuses.

In many places, these schools compete against other large schools in the same location. Schools this large might be divided into several campuses. If you choose to work at one of these schools, there is a chance your children will be in another location each day. Advantages include the highest level of resources available, increased access to technology, and the benefits of living in a large metropolis. On the downside, you will probably not make substantial relationships with school leadership, you might teach just one course, and you can definitely get lost in the shuffle of living in such a large city.

Types of Schools

Schools fall into several distinct categories: association-owned, proprietary, company-schools, and Department of Defense schools. Association-owned schools (in which the parents of the current students own the school) are the most common. They are usually governed by a charter or association agreement and bound to certain statutes such as a nine-member school board. Except in certain countries where association-schools are not legal, most schools in capitals and large cities around the world fall into this category. Proprietary or for-profit schools are much more common today than even five years ago. They can be found all over the world but tend to be clustered in cities that have large populations or are located in certain countries. Company-owned schools are few and far between and may be located in remote areas where minerals, gas or oil are being extracted. Finally, the U.S. Department of Defense Education Activity has schools around world associated with military bases.

Association schools. As noted above, association schools are the most common. Although laws vary from country to country, most have some status with the government such as an association qualification or special charter that allows them to exist. Almost all of these schools have policies that state what they can and cannot do. For example, many of these schools have tax-exempt status, may need to have a local graduation track, or might not allow local teachers to work at the school. Most are made up of board members who are voted on in a general assembly once every year or two or through perpetual voting among the board members.

Change in these schools may take place more slowly than other types of schools.

Proprietary schools. Proprietary schools are scattered across the world, as well, although on a much smaller scale in most areas. Some countries require overseas schools to be majority-owned by host country nationals. Other schools are more opportunistic and hope to generate a profit. Most proprietary schools are owned by a small group of individuals, a corporation, or one person. In general, the salary and benefit package at these schools has a reputation of being somewhat less than association-owned schools although there are always exceptions. Change in these schools can be very swift as a small group or one individual can make the change without any oversight. One should be very thorough when deciding if they want to work at a proprietary school if it is owned by one person. While it should be not a deciding factor, knowing that someone 'owns' the school and is trying to make profit from it should be considered. In the last few years, it seems more and more proprietary schools are popping up in the developing world, Asia, and the Middle East.

Company-owned schools. Company-owned schools are mostly located in areas that have a major impact in a rural area. A company-owned school might be located in an oil field in the middle of a desert while another is located in the Amazon basin where minerals are plentiful. Oil giant Shell operates several schools, including one called Nigeria Liquefied Natural Gas School, located on Bonny Island. The nearest Nigerian city, Port Harcourt, is accessible by boat or plane. More information can be found at http://www.wclgroup.com/school-management/shell.

Most of these schools exist because there is a need for high-quality engineers, managers, and technicians who are needed on site and would be unlikely to go if their families were not with them. Contracts are made directly with the company that is sponsoring the school. A few organizations run several of these type of schools in many locations across the globe.

Department of Defense Education Activity. The U.S. military operates 172 schools in Europe, the Pacific, and the Americas that are known as DoDEA or DoDs (pronounced "Dodds"). Overseas, there are 115 schools, with approximately 51,400 students and 12,000 teachers.
  http://www.dodea.edu/datacenter/enrollment_display.cfm.

Unlike other overseas schools, the students are children of military and civilians serving overseas for the U.S. military. In essence, DoDDs schools are run similarly to public schools in the United States. Teachers are paid on the same pay scale regardless of where they are in the world, contracts are for one or two years, there is a generous living quarters allowance, transportation to and from post is provided, the government will move your household effects (several thousand pounds). In some cases, they will allow you to move a car. Medical and dental are covered, children are given places at the school, access is given to American facilities and goods through a commissary, and in some places children with special needs are able to attend schools. For these reasons, many choose this path rather than the more unpredictable overseas school route. One negative factor is that U.S. federal and all other taxes are taken out of your paychecks. These schools sprouted up after World War II. The numbers have been decreasing in recent years. In 2006, for example, there were 232 schools and 90,000 students.

Office of Overseas Schools. The Department of State is also involved in overseas schools through its Office of Overseas Schools, OOS. While they do not have direct oversight, they support approximately 200 schools in 150 countries that serve dependents of U.S. government employees living overseas. In general, these are schools that have at least one American student from a U.S. government organization attending the school. In most cities, these students go to the same school and receive the vast majority of support. For example, of the fifty U.S. students in Senegal, all but three go the International School of Dakar, a medium-sized association school. The OOS supports schools by promoting best practices and raising awareness of education practices in the United States. This is done through visits to schools by a small group of highly qualified educators.

Teachers Overseas

Overseas teachers can be as diverse as the student body they teach. Many international school websites like to highlight the variety of teachers they have from different cultures and backgrounds. Once digging below the surface, however, you will most likely find that the vast majority of your colleagues are from English-speaking Western countries, host country nationals, and a few other countries. Of course, there are exceptions. Some schools recruit teachers exclusively from English-speaking countries while others require a percentage of teachers from the host country. This is something to consider when selecting a school.

One thing is certain: the faculty will be a diverse mixture of many shades of teachers. For every teacher who has been at your school for more than twenty years, you can count on just as many who are in their first year. Some teachers may have been to six or more schools while others have never moved since arriving at their first school. The following list is a somewhat humorous attempt to categorize teachers based on certain attributes they exude.

The (local) lifer. The lifer is a teacher who has been at the school longer than possibly imaginable, perhaps even before the school was created. Lifers may or may not travel back to their host country very often and almost certainly associate more with their life in the host country than wherever they came from. At first glance, you might think they are from the host country and for that reason they can be a great resource for school-related issues and intimate details about the country that you may not feel comfortable asking a host country national. They may have married a host country national and have kids who attended the school. Some lifers are stuck in their ways and see change, within their teaching style or the school, as an affront to their persona. Do not expect many of them to be at the forefront of current pedagogy.

The (traveling) lifer. The *traveling lifer* has many of the same qualities of the lifer although they may have been to three or more schools in their careers. They know how the system works and they use it to their advantage. Any place you have been on earth, they have spent a month there. Their picture album could be in *National Geographic* and make Ansel Adams cry. Any story you tell, they can match or tell it better with the addition of a coup d'état or lion attack, not out of vanity, but because it really happened. Most will refrain and let you have the stage. Traveling lifers have a very good world view and get along with everyone in the school. They might view you as someone who will only be at school for a few years and be somewhat reluctant to develop a meaningful relationship. Remember, they probably have 200 friends to visit in just as many countries.

The traveler. The traveler has probably taught in more schools than countries you have visited. They can probably tell you how many countries they have visited before you finish asking the question. Travelers are usually young and adventurous. Don't be surprised if they call you in your first weekend in the country to go bungee jumping in some remote village or to visit the seediest district of the city for a cultural festival. You will be their 10,000th friend on Facebook. As far as school is concerned, they don't plan to stay long so they probably won't know about that new policy that a lifer might be willing to break contract over. If there are any teachers at the school that might have tried drugs when they were younger, ninety percent of the staff would pick travelers first.

The retired/second career. When you think of a good ol' teacher from the United States who has probably never had a speeding ticket or jaywalked, think of the retired/second career teacher. This could be completely different from reality, but they have mellowed out from years of teaching in their hometowns. A retired/second career teacher has knowledge and experience that makes him or her a valuable asset. Although they might not have the overseas experience of a lifer or traveler, the retired/second career teacher is the one that everyone listens to at a faculty meeting. They may not really understand teaching overseas, but they know how to connect with students, teachers, administrators, parents, and everyone else through their vast life experience. They are looking for that one last adventure before they settle back home to be with their grandchildren.

The "What am I doing here?" These teachers fell into overseas teaching and are still trying to figure it out. They are always talking about their home country and why everything is not the way they expected it to be. They probably have a decent amount of experience teaching and do not understand how the school does not have a firm policy on acceptable shoelace colors like their last school in the States. They might be either reluctant to talk during meetings or they might dominate meetings. The latter drives almost every other type of teacher crazy. What am I doing here's can go one of two ways: either into a lifer or back to the U.S. There are few exceptions.

The (host country national) local hire. In most cases, host country national local hires are either in the language department, come from a family of considerable wealth or graduated from the school. Some local hires are teachers who have one parent from the host country and another from the United States or another English-speaking country. In this case, they understand everything about your culture and the host country. They would never miss the opportunity to give their opinion about the politics in western Montana or any event in any place in the host country. The chances of them leaving the school are less than zero. They can be your best resource for asking questions about local laws, cable bills, and calling the Internet provider to ask about an upgrade. Tread lightly: if you are asking for favors, there are many others that are doing the same.

The (other/trailing spouse) local hire. Other local hires are either in the country because their spouse has a job there, or they are almost local because they've lived in the country so long. A trailing spouse might have given up a lucrative job to follow their spouse's career. A local hire's spouse might work in the government, military, a Fortune 500 company, or non-governmental organization. Because they are not necessarily there on their own accord, local hires can be somewhat loose cannons and run the gamut from the best teacher you have ever seen to someone you cannot believe has a teacher's license. Generally, local hires have no say in how long they will be there so the school rewards them with a lower base salary and fewer benefits. Depending on their experience, others may view them as a pariah or a savior. Some want to actualize real change while others bide their time until their spouse gets a new job in another country.

The running from something. The running-from-something teacher thinks that by leaving their home country because of _____(insert event), they will be better off. In many cases, this is a divorce. They don't realize it until they've been abroad for a few months, but they've either a) made a mistake or b) made the best decision of their life. If they decide a) they are miserable from the time they get to school until 24 hours later, then it starts again. Nothing can make them happy. The minor problems in their school are exasperated by a multitude that is unimaginable to anyone but them. You might hear them make comments like, "this city is just too clean" or "why isn't there a direct flight from here to Topeka?" I actually had a colleague tell me that one of the cities we were living in was too clean, I'll let you guess which one (Managua, Rabat, Kathmandu, Vienna, Antananarivo, or Dakar). Time or breaking contract, the cardinal sin of overseas teaching, are the only antidotes. If they choose b) they never look back and may not even return your phone calls or emails. They might go from not understanding how to say "two beers please" to intricate conversations with locals within a few months. Next year's crop of new teachers will probably perceive them as a lifer even though they have only been there for one year. The chances of them leaving in the next five years are even lower than the host country national locals.

The ideal teacher. In reality, the ideal school has a mixture of all these teachers. Of all the sections of this book, this is the one I have most wanted to write. In your first few years you will probably learn if teaching overseas is going to be a career commitment or just a brief adventure. A major factor will be the realization that your life is going to be made up of a healthy mix of all these types of teachers. Besides those you live with, these are the people you are going to interact with daily.

Teachers seem to gravitate toward those who are like them and avoid the others unless there is some intrinsic or beneficial reason for mixing. I feel like a combination of lifer, trailing spouse, and traveler. I interact with almost every type listed above although I certainly have more connections with some more than others. As you assimilate into a school, there is no doubt you will gradually find yourself in one of these groups before you know it.

Extra Credit: Don't worry if you feel like you don't fit into any of these groups. When you arrive at your first school you will be seen as a newbie regardless of who you really are. Even though you are probably independent, you will need a lot of help to get situated, even if you are moving to an American school in an English-speaking country. Everything will be slightly different and the more help you seek, the better off you will be in the long run. Let someone help get your cell phone set up so you can focus on those first weeks of instruction.

Relationship Status and Children

Unlike the United States, where your relationship generally has little or no effect on your work life, it does on several levels in overseas schools. For the most part, schools would rather hire a teaching couple than a single, a teacher with one or two kids rather than five or six, and a teacher without a serious relationship back home. Single females might also have reservations about living in certain areas of the world. With respect to gay and lesbian teachers, depending on the school's location and other factors, such as visas for partners, teaching overseas can be difficult. Next, I will discuss in more detail each of the major groups.

A note on children. Having children overseas can be incredibly rewarding and enriching. From a pragmatic level of getting a job overseas, having more than three children will limit you from many, if not all, schools except the DoDDs schools mentioned in the last chapter. Although they may not say it, your children take up three or more seats that could mean a substantial increase in the school's revenue. Generally, schools will provide a free education to your children as a benefit of teaching at the school. Some schools limit the number of children they will allow to be free while others will make you pay a certain percentage after the first or second child. This is worth checking out. Religious or other affiliated schools may be more likely to accept you with more children.

Teaching couples. Overseas administrators like teaching couples for many reasons. They probably have some good experience, they are generally more stable (won't break contract or move anytime soon), and do not cost as much in the long-term. For example, a housing stipend given to a couple may be cheaper than two individual housing stipends. However, this is secondary to the fact that you are probably good teachers with a good amount of experience and they won't need to replace you anytime soon. If you are a young couple, do not be surprised if the school asks during the interview if you are planning to have children. A married friend working in a for-profit school was strongly advised not to get pregnant during her first year at the school!

Married couple but only one teaches. Schools go out of their way to get the people they want. If you are a great teacher with a lot of value to add, then having a non-teaching spouse probably won't be an issue. In many schools, non-teaching spouses are given the opportunity to work at the school as a grade-level assistant, librarian, secretary, or something along those lines. Contracts are written differently from school to school, so if you have a non-teaching spouse it is essential that you ensure your spouse is given basic benefits such as a visa, insurance, flights, moving expenses, etc.

Single teachers. Some schools have a majority of single teachers. Some were never married and have no children, others are divorcees with or without children, and others are in varying degrees of a relationship. Schools can be somewhat skeptical of single teachers, especially if they seem like they may break the contract after a few months or seem to be trying to live overseas as a means of traveling or living their dreams. While these are not bad characteristics, they are perceived and sometimes real. If you are a single teacher, it is crucial that you have a good sense of what you are getting yourself into before interviewing. It is important you exemplify dedication and commitment. If you can't do this, you might need to think hard about teaching overseas. At the same time, this seems to be less of an issue than it did even a few years ago due to the availability of cheap international travel and the advances in technology and communication.

Single females. Being a single female teacher can present its own set of problems. The same holds true for all females or individuals when they are alone. The main concern is safety. Living in an apartment or house can be dangerous for everyone, including single females. It is extremely important to secure your home even if it means installing expensive locks at your own expense. Keep in mind that those living around you probably know and observe a lot more than you realize. This can be a positive or negative. For example, the neighbors might stop a person from entering your apartment when they know you are away for the summer.

The same holds true for walking alone at night or in dangerous or unknown parts of the city. While you may have felt comfortable walking in your hometown, the possibility of being singled out are much greater in a foreign country where you look different, wear different styles of clothing and present yourself differently than the host country's female population. If you get drunk and walk home or get in a taxi in a country where drinking is generally forbidden, the chances of getting assaulted or worse increase dramatically. As well, if you happen to be wearing expensive-looking jewelry, clothing or accessories, you become a target. It is important to protect yourself by taking precautions in what you wear, carry mace or pepper spray, and always plan on moving from one place to another with at least one other person. It is not uncommon to ask others to make sure you get home or have a plan in case something happens. In some cultures, men view women very differently than they would in the United States. Also, there might be certain presumptions about women out alone at night.

Gay, lesbian, bisexual, and transgender teachers. Overseas schools could be characterized as conservative rather than think tanks of liberal change. Funny enough, most teachers I have encountered tend to be more liberal. Anyway, I have definitely worked with openly gay teachers as well as others who have been very discreet by personal decision or necessity. I am sure bisexual teachers exist and I have never seen a transgender teacher. Knowing what cultures are more accepting will go a long way in making your experience more positive.

Teacher Time: LGBT+ Issues by Emily Meadows

Lesbian, gay, bisexual, transgender, queer, and other (LGBTQ+) people have additional factors to consider when recruiting overseas. Allies, too, will prefer a setting that respects and includes all people, regardless of gender and sexuality. Consider the following when evaluating your fit with a potential school:

- **School Policy** – Bear in mind that international schools often determine their own policies, which can differ significantly from place to place. Some schools explicitly prohibit harassment and discrimination on the basis of sex and gender, whereas others do not necessarily provide these protections. Depending on the school, a transgender child may be denied access to the appropriate bathroom or locker room, for example. Ask administrators to ensure that their policy reflects a school of inclusion and equality.
- **School Climate** –The reality is that many international schools function as tight-knit communities, and the people you work with also end up being the people you live and play with. Try to get a feel for whether the school climate is inclusive, or if it perpetuates heteronormativity. Are there out faculty members on staff? Is there a gay-straight alliance? The answers to these questions can provide some insight about whether the school is meeting the needs of a diverse community.
- **Local Context** – Certain countries strictly forbid same-sex partnership by law, some may neither prohibit nor recognize same-sex relationships, and others still might provide more security for same-sex couples than your home country does. The cultural setting of where you will move can impact everything from the ability to go on a date in public to the availability of suitable healthcare for non-hetero/cisgender people. Local LGBTQ+ organizations (if there isn't one, that tells you something, too) are an excellent resource for sussing out whether the area is safe and accessible for all.

Emily is an alumnus of international schools, having attended the Anglo-

American School of Moscow and the American School of Paris as a child. Since then, she has built her career as a professional educator and counselor across the world, serving children and families in France, at the American School of Kuwait and, most recently, at Hong Kong International School. She holds a Master of Education degree in Counseling, a Master of Health Science degree in Sexual Health, and is a current Doctor of Philosophy student in Comparative and International Education, researching LGBTQ+ inclusive policy and practice.

Organizations

Teacher organizations. Most schools have some type of teacher organization. These can either be relatively ineffectual organizations teachers are required to join, to very influential hyper-organized organizations with requirements based on certain variables such as years of experience and status. Some organizations might have certain powers established in their charter. For example, a teacher organization might be able to approve or disapprove teacher evaluation requirements or school calendars.

Before moving forward, it should be stated that there are no international teachers unions and probably will not be for the foreseeable future due to local, international, and school policies, laws, and regulations.

Teacher organizations usually have similar qualities. These groups elect their own members, usually through a voluntary nomination system. It is not uncommon to have one or two representatives from each division. If you can recall your high school student council you will be on the right track as far as abilities and leadership. These organizations can be proactive although it seems they often lead into nagging sessions about administration or policies. If not run efficiently, you can expect people to talk ad nauseam about parking spots or the lack of efficient copiers. Also, without strong leadership, a few people can dominate meetings and therefore the interaction with the administration.

As noted above, teacher organizations can be either very influential to meaningless in a school. Generally speaking, the bylaws from which the school was founded and the type of school will influence the effectiveness. For example, a proprietary school owned by one person is unlikely to have a strong teacher organization while a well-established not-for-profit school probably has a more effective one. There are exceptions and an astute owner should want the feedback of the faculty in order to make decisions. In reality, this is not always the case. In the same stroke, a strong teacher's organization in a well-established not-for-profit school may make a suggestion that is blindly opposed by the school's board of directors. In reality, the line is much greyer although the value of many organizations lies in the fact that they are a place to vent frustrations in an environment where few outlets exist.

Teacher Time: Yes and... by Zane D.

My wife taught me this improv game in which you must answer "Yes, and..." to every question that is asked. I see it as a valuable tool when trying to affect school culture. I first started my international teaching career 13 years ago and a colleague asked me if I could help her create a lesson plan. I replied, "Yes, and when and where would you like to meet to do it?" This quick response immediately created a culture of camaraderie and a caring atmosphere between us that soon rippled out to our students. When a parent at my school asked me if I wanted to run in the morning at 4:30 a.m. I did not hesitate to answer, "Yes, and how long would you like to run?" I still remember the look of amazement on her face when I said YES. This running group of 2 soon blossomed into a diverse collection of colleagues, parents, and people from a variety of sectors and continues to this day. We would train together and travel internationally to compete in marathons and HASH runs. For me this served as great physical exercise and an educational adventure meeting people with different beliefs, values, and perspectives that allowed me to to invite unique speakers to share their knowledge with my students regarding global issues of health, ethics, government, business, environment, and social issues. At one school I showed TED talks each Friday so that students and teachers could have conversations outside of the classroom without the pressure of grades. Other teachers hosted book and cooking clubs, martial arts sessions, a jogging club that met every Friday after school or a happy hour every Friday meeting at a local bar or pub within walking distance of the school. Other members joined softball or football leagues. At one school there was a Talk Tuesday in which colleagues and friends met to discuss a chosen topic of interest. My wife was a part of an improv group that met for drinks outside of school and would then compete against the high school improv on stage for the community. At another school the Director was the lead singer of a band called the Lunch Thief comprised of talented teachers that would entertain at parties for the greater community. The goal is to say "Yes and..." involve yourself in something with purpose and joy enabling you to make deeper connections with colleagues and the community outside of the classroom in order to begin to understand how to foster an all inclusive school culture that shares a vision of caring for one another.

Zane D. is a Spanish teacher at The American School of Antananarivo. He has also taught in Senegal.

Parent Teacher Foundations. Parent Teacher Foundations or similar groups are found in many overseas schools, especially those that are specifically modeled on the American system. They take all shapes and forms depending on the makeup of the parents and teachers. In one school you may have a PTF that is very active, hosts events, and provides volunteers on request. Another PTF might be in name only and have very little real effect. In my experience, the PTFs in overseas schools focus on the parents rather than the teachers.

Overall, if your school has an active PTF, it will be beneficial. They often provide a list of parent volunteers to assist with a host of activities, from helping with a classroom function, judging a contest, or tutoring a struggling student. Outside the classroom, most PTFs hold events such as a gala dinner, food festival, or a community garage sale in order to raise money for the school. In turn, teachers can request funds from the PTF to improve their practice or add a classroom tool. A PTF might donate the furniture to put in a hallway, supply food for a teacher appreciation ceremony, sponsor a speaker, or provide incentives to buy classroom equipment.

Sunshine Committees. Sunshine committees go by many names but have the same basic functions. For a small fee, usually about $20 a year, the sunshine committee will send flowers to staff members, arrange for cards, and the like for weddings, births, and deaths in the family. As well, they often give away raffles at staff meetings, set up pot-luck lunches, and anything else that might improve the morale of the staff. At the end of the year, the sunshine committee will usually 'host' the end of the year staff party and buy gifts for those that are leaving. This is a great opportunity to find the most outgoing staff members on campus.

Extra Credit: Unless you are an experienced overseas teacher, I probably would not accept a major role in a teacher organization in my first year at an international school. By all means, attend and be active, but lay low in your first year until you can fully develop an appreciation for the politics and nuances of the school that may not be apparent at first.

Extracurricular Activities

Extracurricular activities vary primarily due to the size of the school and the location. Schools in large metropolitan areas have many more activities, both hosted at the school and at local venues. As schools get smaller and the location is more rural, the extracurricular activities are usually limited to the abilities of the instructors. Generally speaking, international schools try to offer a plethora of after-school activities for all ages. This is one of the draws for host country national parents looking to get their children involved and expatriates who want their children to have a similar education to the United States or other Western schools. Your participation will vary from having to participate in some capacity to not having to do anything. I think it boils down to how developed the school's program is and where it is located more than anything. Where resources (and instructors) are thin, I have been asked to do more.

Extracurricular activities are American-centric. French schools, which are scattered across the world, typically offer much smaller extracurricular programs. Schools that call themselves an American or international school will almost certainly have a robust extracurricular program.

Most schools will offer programs that are separated by division and occur in the fall and spring with a possibility of programs, especially in middle and high school (secondary) during the winter. You can expect younger students in arts and crafts, organized sports by age group, music, etc. Middle and high school students usually have three distinct seasons with the same sports programs you would find the United States except American football.

Coaching. As most schools are in regional associations, sports teams will practice a few days a week. Tournaments, which usually happen once a season, are in a different country and involve several days. A few times a year, a school might have twenty-five percent or more of its students absent to play in a tournament. Do not expect to be blown away by the dedication of the students on the team or the amount of practices. Many students, even at higher levels, see sports teams as an extension of their social lives. You must constantly remind yourself that you are probably dealing with students from many cultural backgrounds that may not support extracurricular activities.

If you choose to participate or are contractually obligated, you will probably go on at least one trip a year and be required to coach or advise one season. You usually get some type of stipend for your participation, although I would not count on it paying for your travels throughout the year. A wide estimate would be between USD $500 and $1,500. However, if your children participate in activities, the costs associated with travel and expenses will usually fall in your lap. This can get expensive quickly. One thing almost all schools do is set up programs in which a few students from other schools stay with students at the host school. This decreases the cost and relieves a major headache for the chaperones.

Logistics associated with trips can be a headache. In some schools, the athletic department will take care of everything from getting visas and hotels to securing seats on planes and giving you a per diem. In some schools, these responsibilities are dumped on the coach/teacher. Depending on the location and visa requirements of your students, this can be a nightmare. Before a trip to Russia, I had to go to the Russian Embassy six times before being given a visa. Luckily, the embassy was close to my school and I was able to go during my planning periods.

Adding to the difficulties of getting visas, tickets and other expenses may need to be paid well in advance. This can lead to problems. I have seen more than one student work hard enough to make it to the cut off point of buying tickets, then throw in the towel on his studies. Teachers are left in a bind where a student who might be getting a failing grade spends several days on a sports trip because they were getting a C- when the tickets were bought.

Absences associated with sporting events and other extracurricular activities have not gone unnoticed by teachers around the world, especially in the secondary program. A few students might participate in so many sports and activities that they are gone fifteen or more days each year for excused absences. Grade requirements generally dictate that a student can travel to another location if they do not have any failing grades or several grades below a traditional C. I have been amazed to see students traveling with poor grades. This issue seems to be a hot topic in divisional meetings with limited effect. If you teach in a middle school or high school, you can be assured that you will have days when there are so many students absent you will question whether it is worthwhile to cover new material. Some schools limit the number of activities a student can do, but many do not.

Other extra curricular activities. If sports are not your thing, there are many other opportunities. Many schools have excellent music and choir programs, speech and debate teams, Model United Nations, math teams, science fairs, and just about everything else you might expect. Many times, these events overlap sports events although it changes from association to association.

The International School of Dakar is a good example of a robust extra curricular program. The school year is divided into three trimesters for after-school activities, called ASAs. Students in the elementary school can participate in four ASAs per week that last from about 3:30 p.m. to 4:30 p.m. Activities are run from a combination of teachers and local experts. For example, a student might take circus arts from a local acrobatic troupe and papier-mache with a fourth-grade teacher. Students can continue in the same ASA all year or change each trimester. Each ASA lasts approximately ten weeks and costs about $30.

The middle school and high school have a similar program with several ASAs offered each trimester. In addition, students can participate in sports and drama activities. The schedule of practices and rehearsals has been arranged so a student can play a sport and participate in a play.

Teachers at the International School of Dakar are required to lead either two ASAs per year or coach one team. Coaches are compensated and are required to attend the regional tournament. If a teacher runs an ASA, that teacher is allowed to decide what to do. For example, one of the teachers runs a very successful drumming and dancing ASA while a high school teacher does coding with middle school students.

Extra Credit: If you are passionate about something, there is a good chance you can start a club at your school without any hassles. This would be good to propose during an interview, especially if you want to separate yourself from other candidates.

Accreditation

Accreditation is important for overseas schools. According to the New England Association of Schools and Colleges, one of regional accrediting organizations, the purpose of this process is to assess whether a school meets or exceeds established criteria through periodic peer review and self-study. The focus of the accreditation visit usually includes overarching functions of the school such as the mission, vision, and curriculum. Visits take place once every ten years with a small review or update every five years. Schools have initial, provisional, or full status as an accredited school. Being accredited is a big deal for schools, especially at the administrative level, as it provides a level of rigor needed to attract the best teachers and students.

Accreditation visits could be compared to an audit of a school or business in the sense that a group of strangers comes to the school, assesses all areas, and writes a report indicating the school's strengths and weaknesses. More importantly, the group decides whether the school can be accredited. The group is usually composed of six to eight experienced overseas educators or people familiar with school structure and administration. The first two days are spent collecting data, observing classes, attending various meetings, and interviewing teachers, parents, students, and administration. As many staff members put a lot of time and energy getting ready for these visits, expect nervous energy everywhere. The third day is usually spent finishing interviews and planning the written report. The fourth day is spent writing a lengthy report that is presented to the administration and board on the fifth day. In my experience, this has been followed by a full faculty meeting with an executive summary and a question-and-answer session. Depending on the recommendations, schools are expected to improve in areas that have been identified as areas that need improvement.

Your role in an accreditation visit depends on the school. Some schools assign one person to be in charge of the visit. This may be an assistant principal, curriculum coordinator, or someone who has been at the school a long time. Otherwise, the accreditation process will be led by one the administrators. You may be asked to serve on one of the committees formed to prepare for the visit. At the same time, teachers are asked to provide evidence in certain areas. Another thing you might be doing is taking care of some of the recommendations that were expected either five or 10 years ago but never addressed.

Although necessary, accreditation visits have mixed reviews among teachers. In schools with too few teachers or weak leadership, the preparation for the visit may expose gaping holes in the school's function. For example, a school without a working curriculum may task teachers with writing the full curriculum for each of their classes before the visit. Accreditation visits may lower morale and take away from working with students and improving one's teaching practice. They are also stressful. While the end results may be positive, many administrators and teachers look at them as something like a final exam that you either pass or fail. In their view, if you pass you can move forward without looking back rather than building on your strengths and eliminating your weaknesses.

4 Teaching Overseas

overseas school. However, I am sure many questions remain. What are the students like? What is a typical day in an overseas school and how is it different from what I am used to in the United States? This chapter will answer those questions and describe students you will encounter in almost every class. Then, it will discuss English as a Second Language programs, class size, discipline, religion, and the calendar.

Students

Students in overseas schools fall into four categories: host country nationals, short-term expatriates, long-term expatriates, and the children of teachers. Although it is hard to generalize any group of students and there will be students outside the norm, the following paragraphs are some characteristics. Students are influenced by a variety of factors, such as their culture, peer pressure, and many other factors.

A few examples might help. A host country national in Russia would be a student who has one or both parents with a Russian passport. If that student went to school in Japan, that student would be an expatriate. Expatriates are students who do not have parents with a passport from the country in the location of the school. Some expatriates may have been in the school for more years than the average host country national. For example, a child of a teacher might have been in the school for four years while a host country national student may have just started this year. Third culture kids are students who have a nationality but may have never lived in that country or have moved so many times they do feel like they have a home country.

Depending on the country, language ability, configuration of the school, percentage of students in each group, and many other facets, the intermingling between host country national and expatriate students can vary greatly. In some schools it will be hard to figure out who is in what group while in other schools it will be hard to get different groups to speak to each other. It appears that smaller schools tend to have more intermingling because different groups tend to be in the same classes and spend a lot more time together. Large schools might have enough students from different countries to have ethnic groups within the expatriate communities. For example, a school might have a group of students from one country who isolate themselves or are excluded from other students. Another important factor is the percentage of host country national and expatriate students. The more host country national students a school has, the more likely the host country national students will congregate together and speak their native language. This is difficult to manage in light of the fact that most overseas schools include something in their mission statement about developing English-speaking students.

Host country national students usually make up approximately twenty-five percent of your school although some schools have almost 100 percent, while others have none. Many schools have policies that either limit the number of host country nationals in a class or the number of non-native English speakers. If you have host country nationals in your school, some may have been in the school since pre-kindergarten while others may have never been to an overseas school.

Host country national students. Host country national students have some characteristics that set them apart from almost all other students. To get some perspective, host country national students pay full tuition at most overseas schools (although some receive some type of scholarship). Keep in mind that an international school is usually more expensive than attending a public college in the United States. Most host country students are from privileged, wealthy families. Their parents may have highly influential jobs in the government or leading corporations. This is reflected in the host country students you teach. While many will be well behaved and understand the value of their education, some students in this group are spoiled and expect every accommodation possible. Their parents may not always play by the rules and this has trickled down to them. In some cases, both parents may be away from the country most of the time or they are too busy to provide support for their children. I have had students who were essentially raised by a nanny. Luckily, most host country students have supportive parents who expect their children to do well and provide the resources to make sure their children are successful.

One thing to remember is that many of these students have been in the school for a long time and plan on graduating from there. They also realize that many of the expatriate students and teachers will only be there a few years. As such, it seems that many host country national students congregate amongst themselves. Another important point to remember is that as these students get older, they tend to have more access to positive and negative influences outside the school.

Short-term expatriates. Short-term expatriates are those students who are in the country for less than five years. Amazingly, some students are only at the school for a few months before moving on to their next post. More likely, a student will be in the school for two or three years. The U.S. State Department, which has a presence in almost every capital and many large cities, has a policy of two years with an extension for three possible. If you are in a State Department-sponsored school in a large capital, you could expect up to twenty-five percent of the students being State Department dependents. Although the specific details of host country national students and expatriate students will be covered in more detail later in this chapter, expatriate students have some characteristics that separate them from other groups. A good proportion of short-term expatriate students have lived in countries around the world, may speak several languages, and seem beyond their years. Most have parents who have relatively high positions in government, military, aid organizations, and multinational corporations. This is reflected in the expense these organizations pay to have families move to overseas locations. Most have parents who value education and provide support.

Long-term expatriates. Long-term expatriates are interesting in that they are not from the host country but have a deep understanding of the host country's culture and language. For some reason they have been in the country for a long time; this may be because of marriage, personal preference by the parents, business opportunities and just about everything else you can imagine. These students generally have supportive parents who can be great resources. The students can be helpful, as well, because they have one foot in the expatriate community and the other in the host country community. Because students in the short-term expatriate community change so often, it is not uncommon for long-term expatriates to eventually associate more with host country students.

Children of teachers. Children of teachers are their own category as they do not fall into any other very well. Almost all schools around the world provide an education benefit for children. These students may or may not have lived in their parent's home country and may be caught between cultures. Like many of the students in the two groups above, these have been termed Third Culture Kids, or TCKs. Children of teachers have strong academic records and supportive parents. Many of these students are deeply involved in many activities. However, there are some negative aspects associated with these students. Some hide behind the fact that their parent is a director, principal, or teacher. They use this to their advantage. For example, a student of a teacher might regularly skip classes knowing a teacher will not report it. In my experience, teaching children of teachers has been an overwhelmingly positive experience.

As noted earlier, most expats will be children of diplomats, business executives, nongovernmental organizations, military, and children of fellow teachers. Although these students are perceived as only being at the school for a few years, this can be misleading, especially with children of business leaders, children of teachers, some country's diplomats, and some military. Expats come in all shapes and sizes; some may be the only student from a certain country and speak very little English while others have hundreds of compatriots and use English as their first academic language.

As expats are usually very diverse, it is hard to quantify any trends among them. Many expats move every couple of years and do not have difficulty finding friends, adjusting to the school, and doing well. A small percentage flounder and do not do well socially or academically. In reality, the vast majority fall somewhere in between. Expats who have been in the country for more than a few years may be fluent in the host country language, know more about the culture than host country national students, and have many host country national and expatriate friends.

English as a Second Language (or Third, or Fourth)

Almost all overseas schools have extensive English as a Second Language, ESL, programs. Depending on the school's mission and policy on non-English speaking students, the program and services offered can vary greatly. In general, the younger a student is, the more likely services will be offered. It's common to have many students in kindergarten or first grade that do not speak any English, while it would be rare for a school to have a 12th grade student who was not at least close to fluency. Most schools have policies that limit the number of non-native English speakers. In many schools, policies are set (but sometimes overlooked due to financial or political reasons) around ten to twenty-five percent. Other schools encourage non-native students to learn English and might have ninety percent or more students without English as their first language. This is a good question to ask in interviews to get an idea of the students.

There are several ESL models. These range from full inclusion without resource help to full-day intensive English classes with a small group of ESL students. In a full inclusion model, the student attends all regular classes and learns English as the content is presented in English. In younger grades there are several students in each class who are ESL students. For example, a kindergarten class might have twenty-five percent non-English speakers whereas it would be rare to find a 10th grade class with more than 10 percent. In any case, the inclusion model with in-class support seems to be the most common method for new students in the younger elementary classes.

As students get into upper elementary school and middle school, they are more likely to have small classes with other ESL students. A typical program might have students in intensive ESL classes for their core classes, then non-core classes such as art, physical education, and drama with all students. This seems to be quite common, especially for middle school students in medium-sized schools (300+) or more. Another model includes a teacher who assists ESL students in core classes. Although this model works well, many ESL students do not like the extra attention they receive. Some schools have transition classes where students who have graduated from ESL inclusion classes move into intensive writing or reading classes rather than another foreign language.

Most schools have some type of policy about the age or grade of ESL students entering the school. Many schools will allow a middle school student (or younger) to enter the school without English. Having a good academic background would be an important factor. Most schools do not let non-English speakers enter the high school without some English knowledge. It is usually at the discretion of the principal or whoever makes these decisions.

ESL programs in overseas schools are not well researched and use models established by large studies in the United States (with different populations). I am unaware of any studies on ESL students in overseas schools. However, many overseas schools have the resources to offer a strong ESL program. Parents of both ESL students and English students expect the school to provide individual support for ESL programs. Regardless of pedagogy, some parents do not want their children in classes with ESL students and parents with children in ESL programs want small classes where their children can learn English quickly.

Whatever method is used, some students will exit the ESL program quickly while others linger. It seems that students with native languages that are not widely spoken may have more impetus to learn English than a student who is fluent in the host country language. Your school should have regular testing to identify strengths and weaknesses in English acquisition and adjust learning strategies and classes regularly.

Class Size

In my experience, classes in all levels of overseas education are smaller than classes in public schools and most private schools in the United States. Many elementary teachers have a full-time aide or at least one per grade level. You could expect somewhere between twelve to twenty children in each class. Some schools might push that up to the mid-twenties. In middle school, the number might be determined by several factors, including your schedule, the student's schedule, and the number of students in each grade. For example, if you teach in five out of eight blocks, the schedule might work out where you have twelve students in four of your classes, but twenty in another. This could be due to your schedule or the diverse schedule of your students. The twenty students in your one class may be the result of a student taking two languages rather than one. Keep in mind that most administrators try their best to make schedules as perfect as possible. Inevitably, it never works out for everyone. High school classes tend to be smaller, especially as students take IB, AP, or advanced classes. One could expect anywhere from ten to twenty in most classes. This is definitely something to ask when you are interviewed. Keep in mind that smaller classes do not necessarily translate into less work as more individualized instruction might be appropriate.

Assistants or aides in secondary classes are less common. A general rule of thumb might be that if a school can afford to hire a qualified person (think developing country with low wages and many university graduates without employment) or very high tuition fees, you might have an aide. In the six schools I have taught in the secondary, I have had one part-time aide. However, several full-time staff members were available to make copies, translate, and complete other administrative tasks.

Discipline

One of the best things about working in overseas schools is that they are usually private institutions and somewhat selective in whom they accept. At the same time, schools must keep a certain number of students to fulfill budget requirements. Some students seem to be strung along year after year for several reasons. More on that later; let's first discuss the good.

In general, most students will be well behaved. This changes from school to school, region, culture, and the leadership in your division. Most students come from prosperous families or have parents who work or have held positions such as diplomats, business executives, military leadership or positions in nongovernmental organizations that hold education in high esteem. Most expect their children to go to a good university and get a good job or take over the family business. As such, most teachers get support from parents. Leadership is also an important factor. If the principal of your division has high standards and is respected by the faculty, the students will behave better. In my experience, I have noticed that the school leadership is a little more lax regarding discipline policies than in the United States.

For students who misbehave, there are some remedies. In many instances, a quick email or phone call can curb poor behavior. If that does not work, some schools have policies that may be followed. These might include daily cards in the elementary school, 1-2-3 strike systems, and behavior notes on the report card. I am sure there are many other systems that schools have in place to curb poor behavior. You can certainly find out more by asking the person who interviews you. This would be expected and the answers can give you an idea of how the leadership at the school deals with discipline issues.

Dealing with parents and discipline can be a hassle. I have had many experiences with parents who did not seem to think their child's poor behavior was possible. These also seem to be the parents who watched their child do every problem for homework and watched them put it in their book bag and do not understand how you did not give them full credit for turning it in a week after the report cards were handed out. This often appears to have something to do with cultural differences. Explaining to the parents the expectations of the class, citing specific examples that are difficult for the student to refute, and having a face-to-face meeting with the parent and student have been successful.

Extra Credit: When dealing with parents, it is important to remember that different cultures have different expectations for teachers, students, and parents. While you may have been able to use one strategy to deal with a student issue in the States, it might take several strategies within the same classroom overseas.

Religious Beliefs

Religion can be a major factor in some schools and non-existent in others. In some schools, religious ceremonies and holidays dictate the calendar, weekly schedule, values within the school, and even cafeteria foods. In others, religion may not be a school issue but could be very important to individual students.

Although overseas schools are more lax than the average school district in the United States, some things you do in class may be perceived as extremely offensive to some students. Here are few personal examples from my teaching experience. A student refused to participate in a co-ed swim class due to religious beliefs. Another student had an excused absence to meet his guru at an especially auspicious time that conflicted with the school's schedule. Parents did not want their children to see an excerpt of a Harry Potter movie due to religious beliefs.

Extra Credit: If you are concerned about something, cover yourself by speaking to your administrator followed by an email to parents asking them to contact you if they have any problems.

School Calendar

The calendar is usually created through a group of teachers, the board, or administrators with the board voting on the ultimate calendar. It is usually done a few years in advance and might be in a draft version for several years in advance because schools in associations need to plan sporting events and conferences. Some schools, more in the Southern Hemisphere, have their summer break during the Northern Hemisphere's winter. This is less common today but it still happens and can wreak havoc when a child from one of these schools moves to a Northern Hemisphere school. Depending on which direction they move, they are a half-year ahead or behind their class.

Religions definitely affect schedules. Most schools have breaks associated with national or religious holidays. If it is an American school, holidays might also coincide with traditional American holidays. The American school in a city may take off Thanksgiving Day while the international school in the same city may not. Many schools in Muslim countries do not have school on Thursday and Friday or Friday and Saturday rather than Saturday or Sunday. A quick glance at the school's website will usually answer all your questions.

Overseas schools have longer breaks throughout the year and a shorter summer break. If you are new to a school and are required to attend the school's orientation, you might be expected as early as the first week in August. One of my friends had to report to school before July 1 on the first year of his contract for tax purposes! Most schools begin in late August and finish in mid-June. Generally speaking, a school will have a fall break or weekend, a winter holiday over Christmas and the New Year, a break in February, and a spring break. Depending on the number of required days, your school may have all of these or just a winter break and spring break. In some schools, the winter break and spring break are three and two weeks, respectively. This gives teachers and students the opportunity to travel to other countries or home. The fall and February breaks are typically one week.

Here are a few things I have learned over the years. Planning ahead can be a real factor in making the schedule work for you. If you are scheduling a trip home, advanced planning and time to recover from jet lag should be considered. Also, some airlines are notoriously unreliable: they delay flights or cancel them for no reason at all. A friend flying from Madagascar to Bangkok for a job fair went to the airport for a Thursday departure only to be told the flight was delayed until Monday! Ask other people at the school their opinions before actually booking a ticket. Also, nothing infuriates administrators more than teachers who fail to turn up Monday morning because of sloppy vacation planning. A few friends got stuck in Boston at the end of the winter break and missed the first three days of school. They had to take leave without pay even though it was not their fault.

At school, planning ahead can be important, as well. Although this a personal decision each teacher must make, scheduling tests or major assignments on certain days may mean many students are not there to participate. For example, if your school calendar indicates you do not have school on a Thursday in November (Thanksgiving Day), some students will probably be forced by their parents to take the Friday off, so that they can go on a short vacation. Other things to keep in mind are days when many students are on sports or academic trips, choir events, hearing local speakers, and attending events. A counselor at the school in Austria a few years back found that approximately 40 percent of the school days in the middle school had at least some percentage of students with excused absences for school-related events.

5 Living Overseas

Living in a different country will never be the same as living in the United States. In some places, many things will be similar while in others just about everything is different. Regardless of where you live, you will need to figure out how to get along outside of school. The next chapter will outline some major components, such as housing, paying bills, local help, mail, food, and electricity. While paying the bills or plugging your computer into an outlet may seem insignificant, a little local knowledge and realistic expectations can go a long way in making your transition smooth.

Housing

Housing can make or break an overseas experience. A good house should be a respite from the stresses of work and living in a foreign city or town. A substandard house will only add to the stress of overseas life. If you spend enough time in enough schools, you will experience both. In general, categories of accommodations include school housing on campus, school housing off campus, subsidized housing, and non-subsidized housing. All have positive and negative aspects. It is important to understand your school's policies and benefits regarding housing when signing a contract to ensure you have as few surprises as possible when moving into your new abode.

A handful of schools provide housing on campus. This usually consists of apartments or even small houses somewhere on a large campus. In an even smaller number of schools, the apartments may be connected to the actual school. On-campus housing is often offered to single teachers or those without children. Being so close to the school means your commute is obviously short but it also means you are always at school. It also offers the opportunity take care of something at home without ever leaving or eat lunch in your own kitchen. Another benefit is that the school will probably pay most, if not all, your living expenses and might even have your apartment cleaned. On the downside, it is somewhat awkward hosting people at your house and you may have other teachers living next door. Talk about a fishbowl.

Still somewhat uncommon, some schools offer housing off campus that is fully subsidized. The main difference between this housing and the next categories (finding your own apartment) is that you often have more support from the school and you pay nothing or little for the residence. You should expect to pay for electricity, water, phone, Internet, and other living expenses. The benefits are that the school finds the place for you and signs the lease.

Partially subsidized housing is more common. Many schools provide housing money each month to directly hired employees. Since this money is used to pay for local expenses, you can expect it to be paid in the local currency (that may or may not be pegged to international currencies and could fluctuate greatly). In other words, if the local currency changes dramatically, so might the amount of salary you pay in rent. Although finding an abode might prove somewhat difficult, you will likely find something that suits your moods and tastes, better than school-provided housing. With that being said, the school may have less input with the landlord, paying bills, and fixing a broken toilet. Most schools have a list of houses that have been rented by past teachers and will help you get settled.

The last category of housing is that in which you pay all expenses out of your salary. The only true benefit is that you can find whatever type of housing you like and somewhat control the costs associated with the house. Many teachers find housing either very close to school or in the heart of the city. A smaller percentage might choose to live in a more expansive house a bit farther from the city than other teachers. Many new campuses are being built on the outskirts of cities, which means you may find a good deal on housing.

If you have to find an apartment, there are a few rules of thumb. Start asking questions about housing in January and February, when most teachers must decide if they are staying at the school or moving on. If so, inheriting an apartment from someone else can be delightful. Some people set up next year's lease (for a new teacher) and sell large items such as beds and washing machines without either of you having to lift a finger.

Have real expectations about your housing. If you are moving to an expensive city in Europe, you are not going to live in a large house. In remote locations, you might have a house twice the size of your current one and be able to afford a fulltime staff. Keep in mind that the location of your apartment may be the most important factor for safety, commute time, and overall enjoyment. Good luck!

Paying Bills

Getting your chores done may require no time at all, or what seems like every waking hour outside of school. In countries with advanced banking systems, your bills can be automatically deducted from your account on a certain day each month. In other locations you'll spend several hours in line to get money to pay bills. Some schools will send someone on staff to pay several teachers' bills. My advice would be to ask host country national staff how they take care of these things. It may be as easy as filling out a form, giving a wad of cash to someone who waits in lines for you, or doing it yourself.

There are few things that might make this part of your life as stress free as possible. It is important to keep good records, as they might be more reliable than the service. Also, get signatures, stamps, or receipts whenever possible. Having good records and signatures has helped clear up some discrepancies between what you thought you should pay and what the company charged. Trust your judgment and be prepared to be persistent when dealing with local utilities. Keep money aside for paying bills. In some countries, bills may come a few times a year rather than monthly. In Nicaragua, I wouldn't get an electricity bill for several months only to be asked for several hundred dollars at once. I wish I had the financial discipline to save a little each month. Instead, I learned that rice and beans three times a day was not that bad. Finally, know the rules on paying bills. Some places require you to cancel several months before you actually quit using the service. A cell phone is a good example. You may also be asked by your school to leave a few hundred dollars in cash to pay outstanding bills. After a few months, the school will send the difference to your new address or deposit into your bank account.

Cell Phones

Cell phones from the United States are different than phones in most other places. North America and the eastern part of South America use the GSM bands 1900 and 850 while the rest of the world uses 900 and 1800. Luckily, most modern phones are quad band and will work just about anywhere there is cellphone tower. However, if you choose to bring your phone, it must be unlocked for you to be able to use the host country's service. There are online tutorials for unlocking phones, or you might be able to do it cheaply when you arrive in your new country. Also, U.S. carriers have started unlocking phones for you. I was able to buy a used phone from an online retailer and had it within 24 hours. Finally, you can usually find someone to unlock your phone once you move although it could be expensive.

There is probably a place your city that has many shops that re-sell and repair used cell phones. Locals will know where to point you. It might be in the local market, a parking lot, or even a shopping mall. As there are billions of cellphones around the world, it is worth shopping around (if possible) to find the best deal. There are a lot of fake phones popping up in many countries. In fact, I read an article in which people were using real iPhone shells but putting in fake phones. I might even have one in my desk drawer.

When searching for a cell phone service there are several important factors. Most two-year contracts include a decent phone. For example, in Madagascar I could have purchased a two-year contract (for about $75 a month), including a free iPhone. One important factor is the length of the contract and the penalty for breaking the contract. Penalties in some areas may be even more expensive than the monthly fee if you continued the contract until it expires. In many areas, you also must have a written statement (up to three months before the contract ends) to close a contract. Replacement costs are another thing to consider. In many countries, your phone will not hold up as well as it would in the States. Be careful of the plan you get; overage fees can be very expensive and roaming data can consume several paychecks when traveling outside your country. I am pretty sure I have never used my phone enough to justify a monthly contract.

There are alternatives. Consider buying a phone card with limited minutes until you are ready to sign a long-term contract. Some schools have extra phones for sports teams and unfilled positions. Ask the school if they have temporary cell phones for your first few weeks.

Extra Credit: Buy a phone before you leave or get it unlocked before moving. Almost all the world uses the same bandwidth for cellphones today so you are almost certainly going to use yours overseas. It is also easy to buy a SIM card and start using a phone when you first arrive.

Extra Extra Credit: If you do not have the Internet at your home when you arrive, you might be able to get the Internet from your phone using credit. In Senegal, I pay about $10 a month for two gigabytes of data. This really helped in the first few weeks when we were trying to get the Internet at our house.

Local Help

One of the benefits of living in many parts of the world is that you can afford to hire housekeepers, nannies, gardeners, and drivers if you desire. The next few sections outline who to look for, what to expect, and how to ensure you protect yourself and your family.

When hiring local help, it is important to have a structured interview with each candidate. Ideally, this would happen before school starts but not too long after you arrive. It's immensely helpful to have someone buy groceries, get cleaning supplies, and take care of your children in the first few weeks. At the same time, having to fire someone, learn that possessions or money have gone missing, or having your favorite shirt ruined can have a big impact. Like all moves, little things can be more stressful until you get settled. When hiring someone, the most important thing to look for is letters of recommendation from other expats. After that, other things to consider are their ability to speak English, trustworthiness, and overall value. Some household staff may end up being more trouble than they are worth.

In reality, departing expats will probably have a list of people they used and want you to hire. We have been lucky to hire several good people without interviewing. This was based on the glowing recommendations we received in advance and our experiences overseas. In fact, one person we hired to clean our house ended up moving in with us for five years and truly became a part of our family. If you are uncomfortable about hiring someone in advance, just tell the contact at school that you will hire them conditionally for a month or so but want to conduct interviews on arrival.

Paying your overseas help may be complicated. In many of the world's developing countries, a good monthly salary may be extremely low by Western standards. For example, the average salary for a housekeeper in Nepal was between $100 and $150 a month depending on experience, hours, and responsibilities. Obviously, a salary this low in the United States would be criminal. However, in Nepal, where your housekeeper and her family live on approximately $1 per day, this is considered appropriate. Instead of raising their base salary, you can provide benefits such as extra food, health care for the employee and their family (such as immunizations), bonuses for holidays or events, transportation allowances, payments while you are away for vacation or the summer, scheduled increases for years of service and anything else you can think to supplement their income. Of course, occasional raises for exemplary work or specific training are expected if the person does a good job.

Regardless of experience, expect to train your employees and expect some minor mistakes. A few of our wool sweaters are currently being worn by our daughter's dolls. A suit also does surprisingly well if washed and dried only once! While something like theft is inexcusable, you should consider whether ruining a shirt or not mopping the kitchen is worth firing someone. In some places, people have cultural characteristics that are different than yours. For example, in some cultures people would rather tell a small lie than tell you something negative. You might consider this a problem, but remember that you are a guest in their country and they probably do not have any clue that white lies about work-related issues might get you fired in the States.

At the same time, you should never keep someone you do not trust. Clear expectations, written rules and a contract (where possible) can clear up a lot of potential problems. You should be able to dig up a sample contract from your school's front office. If not, embassy communities are good resources. Ask an embassy friend how they write up their contracts for household help.

The bottom line on overseas household help is simple. You want someone you can fully trust with your belongings and children. If you can't, you need to consider finding someone else. With that being said, be considerate that someone you let go is probably dependent on the income you will provide. Their income could provide for their entire family. Many people just need a bit of training and time to do a great job.

Extra Credit: Have you ever heard the saying "don't smile around your students until after Thanksgiving." The same principle applies here; have clear expectations and follow through with your household help in the first few months. If you let small things slide, they will turn into problems quickly.

Mail

Getting mail in a foreign country is great! It is like receiving a little piece of home. In some cases it is as simple as having something sent to your school's U.S. address and waiting for it to come. In most locations you can have something sent by UPS or FedEx and receive it within days. Although this option exists, it is usually very expensive. A friend in the Peace Corps used to receive huge boxes from her parents in the States. The shipping alone was something like $70 or $80 and it was full of items that could be found two hours away in the regional town. What a waste!

Some schools allow you to send items to a central location in the United States. The school then sends it via a cargo shipment a few times a year. Some people use other resources like friends with shipping privileges provided by organizations and embassies for essential items. The director at my last school brought in an inflatable hot tub while my neighbors shipped baby items like diapers. The bottom line is that in today's world you can probably get just about everything you need or want, but it might come at a cost.

Food

Adjusting to the local food will make your life easier overseas. Some people argue that the local food is healthier than a standard Western diet, while in other cases, relying on the local food could lead to dietary problems. Most of my overseas colleagues tend to eat the tastiest of local items and try to cook most of their meals as similar to their home country as possible. In the last few years, I have noticed many cities have superstores similar to the large box stores in the United States. Although they may not have 100 varieties of cereal, they probably have something similar to what you ate in the States.

It is imperative in some locations that you follow the directions of your school regarding food preparation. In some countries, you must bleach or clean all vegetables and fruits before eating them. Failure to do this could lead to serious medical problems. In other places, it is more likely that you will have some minor problems such as an upset stomach or diarrhea. When this happens, hydration should be your top concern. Getting proper medical care if the problem persists is essential.

If you are a vegetarian or vegan, chances are you will be able to eat well. From my experience, produce is abundant in most places. However, everything depends on the season. You may end up eating whatever is available at the time rather than having everything all year. To give you an example, when we lived in Vienna there was an asparagus season and pumpkin season. Some of dishes, like pumpkin soup, were exquisite during those seasons but nonexistent the rest of the year. Many locations also have organic foods, too, sometimes by default. Staples such as rice and grains should be no problem in just about every place on earth.

Water

I took water for granted until I moved overseas. I have found that water is much more important than I ever imagined. In Nepal, our water had to be distilled after being brought in by a truck while in Vienna we had fresh water from a natural spring. Most places around the world do not put fluoride in their water so buy an ample amount before moving overseas, especially if you have children. Tablets are accessible from Amazon and can be purchased before leaving. The safest water is boiled or distilled. Of course, distilling water removes all the good minerals so it should be supplemented. If in doubt, boil your water or buy it in bottled form. In Nepal, a local study found that all but two of the bottled water brands in the country were not safe to drink. Without going into details, I never drank water from a bottle that wasn't one of those two brands even if I was dying of thirst. Never!

Power and Electronics

Taking appliances and other items to another country should not be a major hassle if you know a few general principles about electricity around the world. Your best bet once you have secured a job is to find the correct plug adaptors for the country you are going to before leaving. This can be done through a quick search of plugs for electronics and your host country's name. This will ensure that in the first few days you will able to charge your computer, phone, or other electronic devices.

The power supply in the United States is a bit different than most of the rest of the world. If you are moving to Central or South America, you may not have to do anything as they use the same electricity current, frequency, and plugs as the United States. For the rest of the world, all you may need to do is buy a few adaptors that will fit on your U.S. plug.

The power supply in the United States is 120V (volts) and runs on 60Hz (hertz- or cycles per minute). Most of the rest of the world runs on something different, but almost always between 100 and 240V and 50 or 60Hz. The voltage (V) is very important as a product that only runs on 120V will not work and might cause a fire or trip a circuit breaker and destroy the item if it is plugged in an outlet that is not 120V. The hertz refers to the number of cycles per minute. A product such as a clock that runs on 60Hz will not tell the proper time if the electricity runs on 50Hz. Most of the world runs on 220V or 230V, with exceptions. Regardless, any product that runs on 100-240V and 50 or 60Hz will work almost everywhere in the world. All electronics have a label on the plug that indicates their voltage and hertz.

There are a couple of things you can do now to minimize problems in the future. When you buy products, try to get ones that run on 100-240V and 50-60Hz. This will ensure that they will work when you move overseas. Some products, such as hair dryers and kitchen appliances, might be hard to find with multiple voltages. If so, it might be easier to buy one when you arrive in your new country. My wife and I learned that trick after ruining a few hairdryers and tripping the breaker about a million times. Also, you should do an Internet search and buy a few adaptors. Another option is to buy a few step-down or step-up transformers. Essentially, these will convert a 240V power supply to a 120V power supply and U.S. plug without you having to do anything. Almost all of these also have a built-in circuit breaker that can help in case of unsteady power supplies. These are heavy, about twenty to thirty pounds, and might be cheaper if bought at a specialty shop in your new city. You can also ask your school if they can provide a few.

Power supplies in some countries can be troublesome, especially in the developing world. Public grids may be stretched beyond their limit, lines may be illegally spliced innumerable times, and the infrastructure may be in need of major repair. In old edifices, the developing world, or cheaply constructed buildings you might find that you constantly trip the main circuit breaker, the power from the electric company has surges that can cause major damage, or power is intermittent or on a schedule. In any case, it is a good idea to either store your expensive electronic devices or spend a few more dollars on extension cords with built-in fuses that will trip before a power surge destroys your television, computer, and tablet. Depending on the country and its power grid, this may not be necessary. Many people who decide to live overseas decide to buy 240V electronics and sell them before they leave. As there is little use in shipping them back to the United States, many will sell them for a reasonable price when they leave.

Extra Credit: It seems like you need better than 20/20 vision to read the label on electronic devices to find out if they are 110V, 220V, or 110v-240V. Buy a magnifying glass for checking and label the actual cords with a green string for 110V-240V, yellow for 240V (if you are in a 220V country), and red for 110V only.

Practicing Your Faith

If you follow any of the major religions in the United States, there is a good chance there will be a community of similar believers in your city. Many will have an English-language service at least once a week if not more. It is important to remember that some countries are more tolerant while others have restrictive laws regarding religion. Proselytizing or practicing your faith in public can be illegal in some countries. If you do not feel comfortable asking people in your school, stop by a local hotel and ask what is offered. I have never been to a school or country where I felt people could not at least practice their faith in private; however, I am sure some exist.

Financial Matters

Traveling to and from the United States. Most contracts will include airfare to and from your home of record at the beginning and end of the contract period. In other words, if you sign a two-year contract, they will pay for you to get to the location and get back to the United States at the end of your contract. Dependents will most almost always be covered as well. A family of four should expect four tickets. You will have to negotiate a child under 2 if you do not want them on your lap. Some schools, especially those in very desirable locations, may not include flights either or both ways, but that's unusual.

Many schools will also provide a round-trip for each member of you family over the summers. You get either the cash equivalent of a flight to your home of record for each member of your family or a ticket to your home of record for each member of your family. This is important if you don't plan on returning to your home of record every summer. For example, a friend of mine was married to another teacher whose parents lived in France. The school only paid for tickets to the States, so they did not get the flight to France even though they had to travel through Paris to get back to the States. As I recall, the director of the school ended up giving them cash equivalent of a flight to Paris rather than the United States. Regardless, this might be something to ask about when discussing your contract.

Traveling outside the specified contractual obligations will be on you. Many teachers never take advantage of summers in their adopted country, preferring to depart to the United States the day school lets out and return the day before they must report back. This has always boggled me because the summer is a great time to at least spend a couple of weeks relaxing and discovering your new town.

Finances in a foreign country. Many schools offer a choice of payment. This can be anywhere from 100 percent U.S. dollars to 100 percent local currency. If you have a choice, it seems most teachers ask for their local living expenses to be taken in the local currency and the rest put in a U.S. account. As needed, you can take money out for special purchases, trips, or other debts in the States. Some schools have only one option for all teachers. Considerations also need to be made for the proper banks both in the United States and abroad. Some U.S. banks charge less for transfers and nothing for international transactions while others charge exorbitant fees for both. It is most practical to use the same local bank as the school, so that you can get help setting up the account and have someone to go to when problems arise. It is important to be able to switch from the local currency to U.S. dollars in the event of a currency devaluation. If you are only paid in the local currency and it crashes, you might be working for a lot less than you started working for at the beginning of your contract. This is more likely to happen in countries with unstable economies, frequent changes of government, or heavy reliance on commodity exports.

Saving money. One of the major benefits of living and teaching overseas is the potential to save money. With the recent worldwide recession, it seems like the golden age of saving money might have been in the late 1990s and early 2000s, although there is still a lot of potential. A few couples I taught with over the years had been able to put away hundreds of thousands of dollars.

Jobs are typically offered with the potential amount of savings rather than actual salary. For example, a school that doesn't pay well might say that you will save fifty percent of the salary. Another principal in a school in an expensive city may say that most people are able to save only 10 percent of their salary. The first option may be a better overall deal. Generally speaking, the more expensive the city, the less likely you are to save a ton of money. Chapter 6 describes each region of the world and savings potential. As noted in the first chapter, principals usually do not have any scientific data or actual figures on the percentage of savings possible so take it with a grain of salt.

Taxes. Paying taxes is a fact of life for most people. Many overseas teachers fall into the category of people who pay little or no taxes; it depends on how much you make, where you are from, and where you are working. According to the IRS, if you are a bona fide resident of a foreign country or spend 330 days or more outside the United States in a year and make less than $100,800 (2015), you are entitled to a tax exclusion. Double it if you are a couple. If you are a teacher who makes more than $100,800 a year, please drop this book and call me. I'll be on the next plane to your school. At the same time, if your permanent address is in a state that does not have an income tax, you will not need to pay state income taxes. Some overseas teachers record their permanent address in one of these states solely for tax purposes. For example, a teaching couple I know went to Florida for a weekend with the purpose of establishing residency in Florida rather than Ohio so they would not have to pay Ohio state income taxes. Finally, the country you work in may not require foreign workers to pay local taxes. In other cases this is taken care of by the school. Either way, it is definitely worth checking out before accepting an offer.

There are people available to help with taxes and other financial issues. Check the international trade magazines associated with the job search organizations and regional organizations around the world. A list is located in the last chapter. When I was single, I did my own taxes. Today, my wife and I have hired someone to do our taxes as well as plan for our retirement. Even though we have not made a ton of money we are saving for our retirement with money we would have been spending on other things a few years ago.

The IRS website has a good deal of information and examples. The money saved from not paying federal incomes taxes will almost certainly be more than cost of an accountant. Ask around at school and you will probably find another teacher who knows an accountant that can do your taxes for you. Many will even help you do your back taxes if you forgot to file while overseas.

Extra Credit: You still need to file your federal (and State) taxes even if you make below $100,800. Some accountants will help you do your back taxes if you forgot to file while overseas. I'm pretty sure this would be important when moving back to the States.

Retirement. Many schools offer some type of retirement plan. This is often a percent of your base salary that can be applied to a retirement program in the United States. Some schools may require you to put this money into a 401K and may even match what you put in, similar to employers in the United States. In other cases, the school may give you a percent of your salary in cash and allow you to choose how to spend it. In my younger years, I was able to afford a trip to Mount Kilimanjaro and a safari in the Serengeti with my retirement funds. Oops! While probably not the most pragmatic financial decision I ever made, it was a trip of a lifetime.

Most schools do not offer a long-term retirement plan. It is important that you set something up yourself. There are several financial planners who work with overseas teachers.

Transportation. Your most immediate transportation need will be getting to and from school. A small number of schools offer cars for their teachers. Occasionally, a school will have a small fleet of vehicles that can be used by teachers. Even more schools provide transportation to and from school. This might be a school-sponsored bus or van. In many locations, the school is in a desirable location, so being able to walk or ride a bike may be a great alternative. Another option in many countries is local transportation or taxi. In my experiences in six countries, I took a taxi in Nicaragua, drove my own car in Morocco, either took the school bus or rode my bike in Austria, and rode my motorcycle to school in Nepal, Morocco and Senegal.

Buying a car in a foreign country is a decision you will probably make at some time in your career. In some locations it will make your life easier while in others it might be an expensive pain in the neck. For example, in the Middle East cars are plentiful, gas is cheap, and having a car improves your quality of living immensely.

However, many people ditch their cars at the airport when they leave so they don't have to pay local taxes. In many places, having a car can be extremely expensive and not worth the hassle, especially if your town has dependable public transportation. Even so, I have noticed that most families overseas take the plunge and get at least one car. A new alternative, especially in large cities, is car sharing.

I had never ridden a motorcycle before moving overseas. I have found that riding a motorcycle to school was markedly quicker but not for the faint of heart. I might not suggest this for someone in the first week overseas or someone without any motorcycle experience, but for some it works really well. If you are thinking about choosing this option, you need to buy all your gear before moving, and ship it. Overseas, I have found that helmets are about the same quality of a construction hat. In addition, protective jackets, gloves, boots and the like are pretty much non-existent.

One last note on buying a form of transportation. Do what the locals do. Buy a car that is common enough that you can get parts and mechanics know what they are looking at. My colleagues who have had the most problems with their cars have bought something that is not common in the country, difficult to get parts, and even harder to find anyone who knows what they are doing when they fix it. Spending an extra $1,000 on a car that is common is probably worth it over that car that someone is selling for a really low price. There is a reason, and that is usually that it has been a pain in the neck.

Dependents

Having and raising children overseas is wonderful. You will be surprised how quickly they pick up the local language, adapt to the different culture, and have friends from all over the world. At the same time, some children have difficulty adjusting to life overseas and may become homesick for the comforts of the United States and their friends and families. Based on my experience about eighty percent of overseas children are well adjusted and enjoy living overseas while about twenty percent regress.

Dependents may also include your spouse. As a trailing spouse, I can personally attest to the highs and lows of living overseas without a fulltime job. In some locales, there are incredible opportunities to explore, create, and educate oneself to the local culture. In other places, this might be more restrictive. Having a plan before moving can make the difference. Many schools offer spouses jobs as assistants in classrooms, the library, or other jobs as they are available. However, these are usually not permanent, they can be reduced at any time, and they are not under contract. Another option is taking classes online. There has been an explosion of online education in the last decade with many schools pioneering their online programs via education classes.

From birth to preschool. Having young children overseas is a bit precarious. Many countries around the world do not offer the same medical facilities and critical care needed for young children. Other countries do not have safe options for delivering babies. If you have young children or are planning on having children in the near future, it is definitely worth investigating. From informal conversations with colleagues around the world, it appears many developing countries are starting to build and support at least one decent medical facility that is up to U.S. standards or very close. In fact, all the posts we have been to have at least a few American or American-trained doctors.

Some locations have world-class facilities that may have better service than the United States. For example, my wife and I chose to have our second child in a private hospital in Vienna, Austria. She and I both thought the quality and overall experience were better than in the United States. If you get a job in Bangkok, there are several major hospitals that cater to expatriates and have incredible reputations. Back to the little ones...

It is important to ensure that your small children can have a good quality of life. Getting vaccinations before leaving is important. If they need vaccinations or check-ups while overseas it is worth asking how others have handled this before ending up somewhere where this is not available. These can be expensive and should be considered before signing a contract. Another important factor is childcare.

In many locations there are several childcare options. Among the most popular options are staying at home with little ones, having a nanny, or daycare. Staying at home can be immensely rewarding but difficult. Raising children overseas can be convoluted by difficulty in language, getting to and from locations, and fewer activities available. However, you might find that some cities have more options and outlets for young children. The second option is hiring a nanny. This option is viable in many places around the world. If you can find someone with experience, it can be a lifesaver. Finally, many locations have at least one or two quality daycare centers. I have heard of people who thought the daycare they used overseas was much better than anything they had encountered in the United States.

Young children will develop a bit differently overseas. If you have a host country nanny or choose daycare, the chances of the child learning a different language increase. Researchers believe that learning more than one language at a time increases one's processing abilities. Having a nanny can be wonderful but can also complicate relationships. Some children (and parents) become too dependent on a nanny. My wife and I are a bit guilty of this as we had a live-in nanny for five years. When we finally parted ways, we noticed that our daughter was lacking some discipline and was a bit spoiled.

Elementary. Of all children overseas, those in elementary school usually have experiences most similar to their counterparts in the United States. Academically, classes resemble each other, and social activities include weekend birthday parties, visiting a friend's house, and playing with other children in the neighborhood.

Depending on their age, an amazing trip to a world class historical location may be uneventful. As they age, they will begin to understand the importance of living abroad, although their culture may develop out of their overseas school culture rather than yours. This is important to remember. Trips back to the United States will probably be exciting and worthwhile.

Middle school. Regardless of where you are, middle schoolers will act like middle schoolers. They will have the same triumphs and tribulations that middle school encompasses anywhere. If you are moving overseas with a middle school-aged child, be prepared for the adjustments associated with puberty coupled with moving to a new country. If this is your first move overseas, your child may react in one of two ways: they love it or they just want to get back to what they know. It seems almost impossible to figure this out before moving.

Regardless of how your child reacts, there are important factors to consider. As mentioned above, your child is probably going through puberty, literal growing pains, and the transformation from a child to an adult. This has been termed the rollercoaster years by some leading psychologists. Academically, your child will probably have a language class that reflects the host country. In addition, other classes such as math may be different than your experience in the U.S. From my experience, there is good chance the students in the overseas school will be one year ahead of the average U.S. public school. Many schools offer algebra or geometry by 8th grade.

Making the adjustment to living overseas is important with middle school children. Your local library should have books about your new country. Making trip itineraries to exotic places can help relieve some of the tension. Knowing about the local customs or holidays can be advantageous. Even though you will not be a tourist, buying a travel book such as the *Lonely Planet* is great for weekend getaways. You will arrive a few weeks before school starts and your child can meet and make friends. Ask your principal if they know of anyone in the same age group that your children can meet before school. Keep in mind that while you are adjusting to your new school, your child may feel lonely or even scared in your house until school starts. Planning activities after work and bringing ready-made activities with you on the plane can make the transition easier. Staying connected to people back home will be extremely important.

High school. High schools in overseas schools are as diverse as they are in the United States. Your child may enter a class of 10 or fewer students or a huge class with hundreds of students. Depending on the type of school and the year they enter, your high school-aged child may be required to follow a totally different system than they had back in the States. This might include a different schedule and academic program, and new after-school activities and sports. These changes may be difficult to adjust to, so be prepared for some initial backlash.

Just like your middle school child, your high school child will probably feel strongly about whether they like or dislike living in the new country. In contrast with the middle school child, they will probably have stronger ties to their friends at home and may be despondent and have a bad attitude about moving. This shouldn't last too long. A few weeks into the school year, they will realize that their overseas school is more similar than they thought it might be. The schedule is not that different, in fact, it might be better, the activities and sports offered are very similar, and the academic program offers similar classes. If the adjustment period is prolonged or especially difficult, ask the high school counselor to suggest some activities, students who might be helpful, or other local resources. Getting involved with an activity or meeting the right people can have a huge impact.

Growing up overseas can present challenges for high school students. Many high school activities such as Friday night football games, dances, and evening activities are American traditions that may not translate well overseas. While they might be offered, there is a good chance they will not have the same bravo as they would in the United States. For example, I have never been to a high school basketball game overseas that had more than a handful of parents or students. Besides Islamic countries (and even some of them), alcohol and drugs will probably be more accessible. In many European countries the legal age for consumption of beer, cider, and wine can be as low as 14. Other countries overlook the age issue altogether. Depending on where you live, access to marijuana for high schoolers may be as easy as or easier than access to alcohol in the United States.

Things are probably going to be a bit different socially. Although drinking and drug use are common everywhere including the States, it is different overseas. Whereas a typical high school student in the States may spend a lot of time hanging out with friends at the mall or at someone's house, it is possible that the overseas kid will want to spend time at clubs or discos. Some parents do their best to steer their kids away from this, while others have a more relaxed attitude. One school I can recall, in a country with a lower drinking age, had a champagne toast for the students at prom. While the decision is up to you, I can say from experience that most overseas students who drink tend to have a mature attitude about it and it has never been a major issue.

Staying involved, communicating, and teaching your child to make responsible decisions will be important. Many students choose not to participate in alcohol and drug use. Just keep in mind that it will most likely be different in terms of the law and local and school customs.

Other dependents. In some cases, you might be able to bring other dependents with you. This might include an older child that has graduated from high school, a relative, or your mom or dad. Unless you are able to get a special visa for the dependent, this may prove difficult. Each country has its own regulations. It would be best to contact the school and have the human resource manager or someone look into this for you. I have never encountered this at any of my schools although it is somewhat common with the U.S. State Department. With that being said, it is usually not a problem to have a relative stay with you on a regular passport and tourist visa. Although it differs from country to country, it seems most countries allow tourist visas for up to ninety days. In some locations you may only have to visit another country for one day (or even less) to get another ninety days. In Nicaragua, a few friends would go to the border about every ninety days, cross it, then return the same day and stay another 90 days. Again, local knowledge and guidance will be helpful.

Extra Credit: If at all possible, ask the school or whomever to set up an Internet connection before you move. If not, bring your child to work one day to use the Internet.

Medical Care

Medical care in most foreign countries is much better today than it was even a few years ago. Whereas there are some cities that do not have a decent hospital, it is more likely that your location will have at least one private hospital or clinic that can take care of almost all your basic needs. In emergencies, there are air-medics who can arrive to most locations on earth within a couple of hours. The bottom line is that medical care is more accessible and better than it has ever been. Most schools have a registered nurse or someone at the school who has at least some medical history. Many schools will ask you to complete a physical with a blood screening before the contract is valid. Most schools provide some type of international-level medical care. Tiecare seems to the most popular if you are interested in exploring more about medical coverage in overseas schools.

The next section will give a brief overview of medical care in overseas schools. It should be noted that my medical care has been under the umbrella of the U.S. Department of State as a trailing spouse. As such, I have never used any overseas school insurance although I had it before I met my wife. This section will be broken into four topics: types of insurance, developed countries, developing countries, and pre-existing conditions.

Most schools offer medical insurance for all members of your family. Some pay the yearly premium but it is more likely you will be required to pay a monthly fee. There a few major insurance companies that most overseas schools use, all with benefits and downsides. In some schools, especially those in which you pay a percentage of your salary to local taxes, your medical fees may be taken care of through socialized medicine. The level of care may be similar to the United States, although you can probably count on waiting longer for certain procedures. If you are on Medicare, your coverage stops while you are outside the United States. You should also look into pre-existing conditions and how the school and their insurance provider cover them.

Developed countries will have excellent doctors and world-class facilities. The level of service is going to be the same or better than you have had in the United States. To give you an example, my wife and I had our second child overseas. She has repeatedly talked about how nice the experience was compared to our first child's birth in the United States. She was able to stay for five days, had daily massages, excellent food, and a high staff-to-patient ratio. In fact, the night of the delivery we were the only ones in the maternity ward with three nurses on staff! I have heard of many people traveling or staying in their developed country to have routine surgeries rather than traveling back to the United States. The only downsides I have really heard of are the occasional problems with language and the long delays in getting the insurance money. In many places, you pay at the time of the visit and get reimbursed. This is also true for prescriptions. Be sure to bring at least a few months supply of prescriptions regardless of where you are going.

Medical care in developing countries can be even better than the United States but is more often than not going to be to U.S. standards. In some developing countries, there might be an excellent hospital with U.S.- or European-trained doctors who cater to the expat crowd. On the other hand, there are usually some locations where a visit to the hospital should be a last resort. The hospitals may not be hygienic, the staff is ill-equipped, does not speak English, and may not have training up to par with doctors in the United States. A friend of mine went to the hospital in a small city in Nicaragua only to leave once he saw the inside. He wanted to get stitches for a cut on his hand but realized he could wait a few hours until he could get to Managua, the capital. I recall him talking about a gurney in the hallway with bloody sheets.

In most large cities around the world, even those at the ends of the earth, there are usually one or two American or European doctors who can assist with most routine medical issues. If you are accident prone or worried about medical care, this should be a consideration.

Prescription medications should also be a concern before moving. Talk to your doctor before leaving and make sure the prescriptions are available in the country you are moving to, or can be mailed. Medications can be cheaper overseas and pharmacists often don't require a prescription. In fact, in some countries, you can call a pharmacy and have a prescription delivered! While less expensive, there are dangers, as well. Billions of dollars worth of counterfeit drugs are sold to unsuspecting consumers every year.

Property Insurance

Even though you are leaving the United States, you should consider your insurance options. The easiest way to protect your belongings overseas is to have them covered under your homeowner's insurance from the United States. This would prove difficult if you do not own a home in the States. In that case, shop around to cover your belongings in storage in the United States and overseas. If you have a parent or a spouse in the military, I would definitely try USAA. Be sure to ask for a policy that covers both living overseas and transporting your items to and from the United States. A lot can happen between points A and B. I have heard of teacher's losing their entire container of goods while in transit. If no one indicated they they would cover the transportation, you probably won't get your shipment reimbursed. Once your shipment is in the country, it can still take a few weeks to actually arrive. In extreme cases, it can take months. In Senegal, one person waited something like four or five months to get their car actually delivered due to 'problems' with the paperwork.

You can also buy insurance in your new country. For about $150 in Austria, we were able to cover up to $20,000 worth of items in our home with a small deductible. A friend of mine had about $10,000 worth of electronics stolen from his apartment and was reimbursed within days. Ask your new school for advice about local insurance.

If you have a car, you will almost certainly need to buy insurance from a carrier in your host country. I have found that in all the countries we have lived, the insurance rates were much less than in the United States. Some expats buy coverage from both a U.S.-based provider and a host-country insurer. It's a good idea to get an international driver's license before moving overseas and the host country's license upon arrival. Some countries will not issue a local license unless you turn in your U.S. driver's license. If you stay in a country for more than a certain amount of time, you may be required to acquire a local license, although enforcement is often pretty lax.

Passports and Other Important Documents

There are many considerations regarding important paperwork when moving overseas. I am sure countless teachers have considered whether they should bring their marriage certificates, birth records, deeds, titles, and other important documents. One must consider the chances of needing to use them with the chance of having something happen to them. In general, I would suggest anything that you may need immediately such as a birth certificate, marriage license, immunization record, medical documents, and passport you should hand carry with you on the plane. Other documents, such as a property deed, you can leave in a joint safety deposit box that someone can get to if needed. FedEx or other shipping companies can get something to you in a matter of days.

A couple of quick measures can ensure your documents will stay safe. Local knowledge is important. Some schools may ask for documents like a passport and other records in order to get a visa. Make copies of all the documents you can and get them notarized if possible. Your U.S. bank can notarize everything, likely for free. If not, the consular section of the U.S. embassy will do it for about $25 each document. Have a power of attorney and living will prepared by a lawyer. Although I am not a lawyer and do not want to provide legal advice, there are two types of power of attorney available. The first is a general power of attorney that covers everything. A specific power of attorney gives someone the right to handle issues related to a single issue, like selling your car. Be careful what you decide and pick someone you completely trust. If you have not filled out a will, be sure to do this in case the worst should happen.

Secure your documents carefully. Some people choose to store their important documents at school (where there is likely 24-hour security), others keep them in safes at home, and some store them in a shoebox in their closet.

Language Classes

Learning the local language can be one of the most liberating aspects of living in a foreign country. If you know another language, moving to a country that speaks that language will improve your experience. Although everyone says they are going to learn the language, only a small portion ever truly become fluent. In reality, the vast majority of teachers learn a few phrases and words in their first few months in a country. After the newness of living overseas takes hold they remember the most important things such as food, directions, and money. It takes several years of speaking a language all the time to be fluent. In some locations, learning the local languages will be essential; in others, the entire country might speak English.

A language class is a great idea if you are highly motivated and have the energy. Speaking Spanish in Nicaragua helped at school and in my personal life. I did not feel the constant pressure or strain of riding in a cab, asking where the shampoo was located, or speaking to parents and faculty who did not speak English. If learning a language were not so difficult, I would certainly try my best to learn the language of every country I have been in. Be realistic and remember that you will be busy with school, discovering a new city, and adjusting to living overseas.

There are several good ways to learn a host country language. I am a firm believer that immersion is the best way. Unfortunately, this will be impossible if you are in an English-speaking school. However, you can choose to spend all your free time immersed in the local culture and learning the host country language. Your next best bet is taking a class with a small group of learners. Many overseas schools will offer introductory classes for incoming teachers. This can be nice because the school pays, the instructor usually comes to the school, and sessions are scheduled right after the final bell. If the school does not offer anything, you can always take classes on the local market. Look for programs that have a curriculum and materials, a large client base, and do not require a large up-front payment. More expensive, individual classes are ideal, especially if you can choose the location and schedule.
 Finally, there are software programs, books, CDs, websites, and other outlets for learning a language. This could be a good starting point to see if you really have the interest in learning a language. Language classes are a lot like gyms in that most people are eager when they sign up but lose interest quickly due to the difficulty of the task.

Safety

Safety in a foreign country should be a top priority. Many countries are very safe and do not require much more vigilance than you would need in the United States. Other countries are much more dangerous and require constant security. Most countries fall somewhere in the middle. Regardless of where you go, you will be a target for petty crimes such as pick pocketing. Vigilance and a few preventative measures can make the difference.

In most countries, you will not have any major security issues. However, it is important to be aware that even though you think you fit in, there are people who can immediately identify you as a foreigner. It may be your shoes, haircut, the way you walk, the dialect you speak, but something is going to give you away.

A few common sense measures can make the difference between enjoying the country and the hassle of canceling your credit cards, applying for new documents from abroad, writing police reports, or worse. First, as much as you can, be aware of your surroundings and avoid lightly traveled areas; instead, try to stay on the main roads or tourist tracks. Even though there may be more pickpockets, the chances of being singled out are less because they will go after the easiest targets. Try to keep all belongings including your purse, bags, wallets, cell phones, and other items in front of you rather than on your back. It is a lot harder to steal a wallet from the front pocket than from a backpack. Walk with confidence and always act like you know where you are going even if you do not. This is especially important in train and bus stations, airports, and other transportation centers. Politely tell the person 'no thank you' the first time they ask for help, and then get stern or ignore them. This is a good time to use your teacher voice! I sometimes dangle my keys at hustlers to indicate that I have a car or a home in the location even if I don't. I am not sure why but wagging my index finger also works more effectively than anything else.

Most places have registered taxis; use them all the time even if other options are cheaper. Of all the problems I have heard about regarding security, using unregistered taxis has been the biggest mistake people have made when living overseas.

Some markets have people who will show you around. In some cases this can be an excellent way to navigate the market and not get hassled by vendors and other guides. Negotiate a price before you begin and pay them at the end.

Other than this, let common sense dictate how you move around a city. Flashy jewelry or clothes should be left at home, avoid dangerous parts of town, always carry a cell phone for emergencies, and let someone know where you are going. The U.S. State Department has files on safety for every country on earth. Read the file and the updates regularly. Check the websites of other embassies, as well. The United Kingdom and Australia, among others, regularly post security warnings. Finally, if you are a U.S. citizen, register with the U.S. consulate when you arrive. The Smart Traveler Enrollment Program, STEP, will send emails or messages as needed, provide updates, and can help in the event of an evacuation. Enroll in the STEP program when visiting any country during your time overseas. If something happens, you will get some type of communication via text or email. However, an ancillary benefit is knowing that someone knows where you are during your trip.

Much more vigilance is needed in more dangerous countries. In some countries you should avoid public transportation altogether. In others, it may be safe to call a taxi but you should never hail one from the street. Traveling at night should be as limited as possible, while some areas of the country or city should be avoided at all costs. In some countries, you should never travel by yourself and always leave your whereabouts with people you trust. Years ago in Togo, a missionary was killed during a carjacking because he 'spoke the language' and tried to negotiate with the guy carrying the gun. Got killed. Schools should provide security briefings and guidance as needed.

If you drink in any foreign country, you will become a more likely target. Besides using unregistered taxis it seems like a lot of people, especially new teachers, get into trouble when they drink too much overseas. They may lose their wallet, have a missing credit card, or get duped by a local and not have much control. If you decide to drink it is important to have a designated non-drinker and a plan for the entire night. Bad decisions can lead to major problems. While enticing, avoid locally produced moonshine or any liquor that is not regulated. A quick search on the Internet will report on deaths from illegal moonshine in foreign countries. This occurred more than once when I lived in Nicaragua.

Here are a few personal encounters I have had while living overseas. In Nicaragua, I did not have any incidents. However, a teacher who had been drinking was kidnapped a few blocks from his house and driven around the city for a few hours while his debit card was used three or four times to extract the maximum amount possible. In Morocco, two teenagers distracted a group I was with by asking for water while one kid took my wallet, phone, and iPod out of the car. We were only ten feet from the car, sitting on the sidewalk when this happened. About a week later, my camera was stolen from my backpack on public transportation in Brussels. I thought the guy was trying to steal my phone, only to remember I had left my camera in an outside pocket for about twenty minutes. He coughed on me while sitting in the seat next to me and successfully stole the camera. I did not encounter any problems in Nepal although several people had their wallets stolen by groups of young kids. One college student on an official visit had a reaction to some drugs he bought on the street. In Austria, nothing happened although home invasions were a big enough security threat that the U.S. Department of State raised the level of security. In Madagascar, the only violence I heard of occurred when people were traveling between cities at night. In one case, a nun was shot and killed over a $20 loan she gave to a Malagasy. In Senegal, a few people in the school community have been robbed while running, walking, or sitting at the beach. There have also been more than a few home invasions. It should be noted that ISD in Dakar provides night guards, which is usually enough of a deterrent.

Police are often not always of the right side of the law. After completing the Peace Corps, I was adamant about not giving bribes to police. Now, I would not hesitate. Police can take your documents, shake you down for whatever they want, and hold you for as long as they want. Best to give them some coffee money and move on. If you really feel incensed, you can report the harassment to the regional police commissioner's office.

While most people would do this anyway, say hi to all the guards near your house on a regular basis. If you can learn a few phrases in the local language it might go a long way in not getting robbed at home. I have heard of more than one person suspecting the guards of being the thieves. While I don't have any solid evidence of this, I would bet most of them did not recognize the guards in the neighborhood as they drove into their compounds each day.

Since the incidents in Morocco and Belgium, I am much more aware of my surroundings and do not shy away from asking someone to step back, or leave me alone. I am loud if I need to be and find a hotel or police officer if someone just won't let it go. This has only happened a few times.

Extra Credit: In my experience, the most-frequent targets of violence are experienced teachers who let down their guard because they feel comfortable in situations that a tourist or newcomer would think were dangerous.

6 A closer look at regions throughout the world

Writing about different regions of the world is difficult at best. It is hard to summarize regions and the schools within them without offending everyone. I will try to provide the most accurate description of general characteristics, including some pros and cons. Keep in mind these regions and their schools can be very diverse.

South and Central America

Many schools in South and Central America are located in large cities. With a few exceptions, the populations are overwhelmingly Spanish speaking and Roman Catholic. In Brazil, the largest country in South America, Portuguese is spoken. When compared to other regions, tuition fees tend to be lower. This is reflected in lower teacher pay and benefits. In general, the lifestyle is relaxed and people enjoy having a good time even at the expense of making money. Access to the United States and its products is easy. You can expect a lot of host country students and administrators/teachers in many schools. Graded (www.graded.br)

in Sao Paulo and Nido de Aguilas (www.nido.cl/) in Santiago have traditionally been sought after by my friends. I taught at the American Nicaraguan School (http://www.ans.edu.ni/) in Managua.

Caribbean

Schools in the Caribbean are similar to the rest of the Americas in terms of lifestyle, religion, and culture. However, you can expect smaller cities and schools. Benefits and pay are similar to South and Central America. Access to water is omnipresent, although coastal tourist resorts are expensive. One school to keep on the radar is the Carol Morgan School (http://www.cms.edu.do/) in the Dominican Republic.

Western Europe

Most schools in Western Europe are elite institutions catering to the wealthiest host country students and the students of experienced diplomats and businesspeople. Most schools have modern, purpose-built campuses and loads of technology. Of all the regions, Western Europe is most similar to the United States, but there are differences, as well. Schools attract experienced teachers and provide good pay and benefits. However, life in Paris, London, and other European hotspots is expensive. While you may have great Internet service and many of the conveniences you had in the United States, you may not be able to afford them. Access to the United States is relatively easy with cheap flights to most major U.S. cities. You can also expect to get enough visitors from the States that you might consider squeezing into that apartment with an extra bedroom.

Some overseas teachers end up not liking Western Europe because they thought it was going to be a carbon copy of the United States and it is not. However, if you want to look at some of the premier international schools in the world, just type in the name of the city and International school. I was a long-term substitute teacher and did my PhD internship at the American International School (http://www.ais.at/) in Vienna. It is a great school and a great example of how good life can be teaching overseas. With that being said, many schools in Europe would be more likely to take a teacher who has already been overseas than taking a chance on a new overseas teacher.

When thinking about living in Eastern Europe I often think of words like 'exciting' and 'possibility.' Schools and cities are changing rapidly. Small schools that were in city centers are moving to larger campuses on the outskirts of town. The pay and benefits are generally less than Western Europe but you can save more because the cost of living is lower. There is access to many imports from Western Europe although they might be a bit expensive. The schools cater to a growing middle and upper class of host country national students although many schools will be mostly expatriates. Check out the Anglo-American School of Moscow (www.aas.ru). It has 1,250 students from over sixty countries including a student from one of my former schools. I just saw his picture on the website home page.

Africa

Living in Africa is difficult but can be incredibly rewarding. Many new teachers I have met started their careers in an African country and have since moved on. Unlike schools in most of the rest of the world, only a small percentage of students will be host country nationals. Larger cities in more developed countries will not follow this rule, but generally speaking this is true. You should be able to save a good portion of your salary while experiencing cultural activities that are completely different from the Western world.

On the negative side, parts of Africa are isolated and dangerous. Travel may difficult or impossible at certain times due to natural disasters, strikes, and political turmoil. Another downside to living in Africa is the extreme poverty in many areas. High-quality medical care is lacking in many African cities.

at the three schools I have taught in might give you a good example of what schools are available. I taught at the Rabat American School (www.ras.ma) in Morocco in North Africa, the American School of Antananarivo (www.asamadagascar.org) in Madagascar, and the International School of Dakar (www.isdakar.sn) in Senegal. At each of these schools there were a lot of people that loved the city and school and a small, but vocal group of teachers that could not handle it. Anything in sub-Saharan Africa should not be taken lightly.

Teacher Time: Sub-Saharan Africa is a Gem...by Lauren K.

I agree that many countries in Sub-Saharan Africa can be volatile but as an African citizen it makes me sad to see all the counties lumped under one umbrella. I come from South Africa and have taught there as well. Transport and services such as busses, Uber, trains and taxis are easy to come by and clean and safe. Health care is great albeit expensive. However, schools usually provide health insurance and then access to health care facilities is easy. There is a lot to do in South Africa. I taught in Johannesburg and there was hardly a weekend that passed without some fantastic event. And South Africans are very friendly people.

Tanzania is a well-developed country with big cities and extensive transport systems. As a foreigner it is very expensive to do things that you might be used to. But once you have your residence permit, life becomes considerably cheaper. The internet is fast and inexpensive in Tanzania and where I taught, at the International School of Zanzibar, wifi was readily available. We even had it in our house. While a little bit more negotiation and preparation is needed in Tanzania, it is a relatively easy country to live in and access to South African chain stores makes buying nice food and other goods easy.

Lauren started teaching Grade R (6 year olds) in Johannesburg, South Africa in 2014. This is her favorite age group to teach. The next year she taught 4 year olds briefly and then moved to the International School of Zanzibar, teaching Year 6 (11 year olds). She thoroughly enjoyed the new level of dialogue she could use to engage with her students. Lauren became involved with international schools after a friend alerted her to an opening in the school. She had previously lived in Zanzibar.

Middle East

Many teachers take jobs in the Middle East and end up loving them. Many cities, especially in the Gulf region, have huge expat communities. Some compounds have tens of thousands of expats living there with American grocery stores, cinemas, and fast food joints. You should be paid well and be able to save a lot of money. Flights to Asia, Africa, and Europe are readily available and affordable. However, there are some drawbacks. Some schools are dictatorial and owned by host country nationals. Some schools have many host country national students who may not be the best behaved and there is little you as classroom teacher can do about it. Of the teachers I know who worked in the Middle East, they seem to be the most decisive regarding whether they liked or disliked working overseas. Based on the number of years they stayed, I'd venture to guess most really liked it.

The Middle East is a global leader in the demand for English-language international schools. A report by the International School Consultancy said the United Arab Emirates now has several hundred schools, with more planned. Saudi Arabia and Qatar are also trending upward in numbers, the report said. This might be a real opportunity for someone trying to get their feet wet in international education.

(http://teachuae.com/middle-east-leads-global-growth-of-
international-schools-market/)

Southeast Asia

Southeast Asia includes all the countries in Oceania, east of India
and south of China. There are a lot of countries in this region so
making general statements is difficult. The large cities will have
schools similar to other large cities around the world. These cities
will have many opportunities both in and out of schools. If you are in
a travel hub such as Singapore or Bangkok, you'll find cheap travel
to a host of countries. It seems like most people are able to afford a
lifestyle better than the average teacher in the States, travel on
breaks, and even save a bit of money. Language issues may exist
more than in other places around the globe as English may not be
spoken as much outside the major cities and the host country
languages are quite different.

South Asia

South Asia includes the Indian subcontinent. India itself has an
expanding English-speaking middle class. Many people who could
not have afforded an international school just 10 years ago are
eager to have their children learn in premier schools such as
American overseas schools. Alongside the middle class and
wealthy, you will see poverty on the streets. More than other places
I've lived, some people love the Indian subcontinent and stay their
entire careers while others cannot wait to get out. The pay seems
to be on par with developing countries and some schools offer
excellent salaries and benefits. Countries in this region tend to be
finicky about visas and many schools favor couples over singles.

East Asia

Japan, South Korea, China, and Taiwan make up East Asia. Many of the established schools offer great contracts and benefits that are rewarded by hard work and long hours. Although I have never worked in East Asia, the people who do talk about two things: the sheer amount of work (pressure) and the amount of money they saved. You can live cheaply and save money while maintaining a great lifestyle. Access to travel and language issues are heavily dependent on where you live. For example, a school in western China is going to be different than one in Tokyo.

China's international school market is booming, largely because of the country's growing middle class. Chinese parents want to send their children to high-profile universities, usually in the United States. That's led to a growth of international schools. In 2014, more than 177,000 students were enrolled in international schools in China, with eleven percent annual growth predicted in coming years, according to an article in the South China Morning Post. (http://www.scmp.com/business/china-business/article/1855932/chinas-booming-international-school-business-untouched))

It's also worth noting that China is the largest source of international students studying at U.S. colleges and universities. China sent nearly 275,000 students to the United States in 2013-14. That number represents 31 percent of all international students, graduate and undergrad, in the United States. China's share will grow to 40 percent by 2017-18, according to an annual report by the U.S. government's International Trade Administration.

(http://trade.gov/topmarkets/pdf/Education_Top_Markets_Report.pdf)

7 Getting Hired

Getting your first job overseas can be a harrowing experience. I was lucky because I was already in Nicaragua, contacted the school and had an interview on campus. Most people today attend one or more of the job fairs in the United States, although there are fairs abroad, too. After one year teaching in Nicaragua I went to a job fair in Boston, spent a few thousand dollars, and did not get anything. I finally found a job using an online job site, called tieonline. More on that later. Since getting married, I've found jobs by emailing schools and interviewing online. This chapter will lay out a plan to land a job by discussing what you can do now, how to prepare and succeed at job fairs, professional qualifications, interview questions, what to look for in a contract, and accepting a job. Chapter 8 covers what to do once you have secured a job but have not left yet.

Overseas Job Cycle

Before we begin, let's spend a moment discussing the timeframe for most schools. The academic year typically begins in August and ends in June. Teachers usually must decide before the December break whether they want to return for the next academic year. Of course, some people know beforehand they are not coming back and a small group get extensions for various reasons. Job fairs usually start in Asia in December and move to Europe and the United States in January and February. Most of the hiring is completed by February. There is a small spike over the summer if there's an unexpected hike in enrollment or if teachers decide not come back for various reasons, such as medical emergencies. Overseas teachers start contacting schools as early as October although serious discussion does not usually take place until late November or early December. Realistically, you should register for a fair in the fall and begin contacting schools as positions open. You will most likely send an email to a specific address like jobs@overseasschool.com. This email will be routed to the division-level principal. If a position is not open many schools will simply delete your email.

How To Prepare

You need to start preparing now for your next move overseas. If you have traveled overseas farther than Cancun, Canada, or Paris you are probably ahead of the curve. Most administrators would rather hire someone who has lived abroad and has already taught in an overseas school. The perception is that these people will take less time to adjust (hence, more focus on teaching) and they are dependable. Keep in mind that schools invest a lot in you before you start teaching. However, even the best schools with hundreds of applicants for each position will hire the best person for the job, even if they are more expensive. Hopefully that is you. Luckily for all of us, overseas schools are increasing exponentially. According to International School Consultants, there are over 8,000 English-medium overseas schools including 2,000 with IB programs. Getting prepared with documentation, adjusting your activities as needed, rewriting your resume or curriculum vitae, and getting recommendation letters are all things you can do right now. A curriculum vitae, or CV, is a far more comprehensive version of a resume, although it is synonymous with a resume by the British and Canadians.

Documents. You need a passport. Although technically you could get a passport expedited within a few days or weeks of traveling, it is much less expensive and easier to do it now. Since the requirements change periodically, the best place for information is the travel portal on the U.S. Department of State's website. If you do not have a passport, a school administrator who might potentially hire you will see this as a sign that you are not really interested or lack the drive to work overseas. It also shows that you have not traveled overseas (or not in a long time). Getting together other important documents such as wills, power of attorney, birth certificates, and other legal papers will help alleviate stress once you land a position. Although you may not need these documents overseas, you do not want to spend your already frenzied last week in the States trying to find them.

Activities. Another thing you can do is start or continue with extracurricular activities at your school. If you coach three sports and direct the play each year, you are in great shape. If you do not participate in any extracurricular activities, you have some work to do. Most schools look for people who can coach or advise extracurricular activities. Even if they do not offer exactly what you are doing in the States, overseas schools like teachers who extend beyond the classroom.

Most activities in U.S. schools apply to overseas schools but not all. For example, few schools have American football. Depending on the size of the school, the association in which they are in, and the level of interest, an overseas school might appear to be similar to a school in the United States. In the elementary school, you can expect a robust after-school program that includes some type of sports mix, arts and crafts, and extensions of curricular related work such as a science club. As students move to middle and high school, there will be a plethora of activities and sports. Being able to coach a variety of sports or lead activities will definitely be an advantage. Many contracts require that you participate in or lead at least one activity. Other schools offer generous stipends then cajole or harangue you until you participate. One of the highlights of coaching a team or leading certain activities is that you will be likely to take the students to another country to participate with other schools in some sort of competition.

CV/Resume/Recommendation Letters. Now is also the time to get together your resume or CV, recommendation letters, and general cover letters. It also is a good idea to think about your philosophy of education and join an organization or two. All these things will not only improve your prospect of teaching overseas but also be a good practice in reflecting on your strengths and weaknesses. You should create a short resume (one or two pages) that you can send in an email. At the same time, write a CV with more detail that can be provided once a school has shown some interest. Most school administrators are extremely busy and will probably decide if they want to hire you based on what you can show in a one-page resume.

Recommendation letters and reference calls are extremely important. Keep in mind that the school that is hiring you may be on the other side of the world, literally. Making a reference call is probably going to be the last step before they make an offer. Besides the information you provide them, this is their one chance to see what you are really like. Highlight experiences that would be beneficial to overseas schools so the administrator includes them in the reference letter.

Depending on who you work for and the circumstances of your current job, tell the administrator who is writing your reference letter what you are planning to do in the future. Highlight experiences that would be beneficial to overseas schools so the administrator includes them in the reference letter. This includes leadership positions, innovative classroom activities, experiential education, thematic units, travel, and extracurricular activities. This includes leadership positions, innovative classroom activities, experiential education, thematic units, travel, and extracurricular activities.

Finally, prep your principal or other references before you attend a job fair. Sit down with them for 10 minutes and explain what you know about overseas schools. Not only will this be good for you, it will provide your principal with some basic knowledge. You could even loan him or her this book for a few days. The bottom line is that you want the reference to show to your future administrator why you are serious about moving into overseas education. The more knowledge the reference has, the more they can help you. Be sure to explain that reference calls may occur outside work hours due to job fairs occurring on weekends and in different time zones. It might be best to ask your current administrator to give their cell phone number rather than school extension. In all likelihood, reference calls will be made outside regular school hours.

Job Fairs

As a teacher moving into overseas education, you will probably attend a job fair in the United States to get your first job. Just like you might expect, job fairs are stressful. Hopefully the fair will include several interviews. I am first going to describe a job fair in generic terms, then provide some advice on getting the best job available.

Jobs fairs are usually two or three days long and held in the conference rooms of a large metropolitan hotel. A few days before you arrive there will be a final list of schools and positions available, sent via email or accessible online. The first night will include some type of reception or dinner and a chance to meet and greet. The next day, teachers will have an opportunity to speak briefly with administrators at schools that have jobs available. In other words, you will have about two or three minutes to convince an administrator to give you a longer interview.

Let's pause for a moment here to think about how to get your message across to the administrator in just a few minutes. Make sure you have a firm handshake and a copy of your resume handy. Give the person a chance to preview it for a second before blurting out how great a teacher you are. Besides getting an interview by discussing your education history, it is important that the person on the other end has something to identify you with. For example, you might want them to remember you as the "former country club golf pro" who decided to hang up the clubs for a different type of education, or the person who spent six months living in the middle of the Amazon rainforest. In my case, I wasn't a golf pro and didn't live in a rainforest so I'd probably focus on the length of time I've been overseas and my adaptability. My current director told me a story of the time his school was opening a new campus and had to hire over 90 teachers!

For some administrators, the only thing they may care about is how well you can do in the classroom. You can typically judge how a follow-on interview will go based on the questions they ask in the first few minutes. If each question is related to school, you can expect more of the same during the next interview. If the person asks questions about your personal life, the same will hold true.

Anyway, after a few hours of this process with lots of schools, you should have several interviews set up. These interviews will be conducted in the conference room itself, the administrator's hotel room, or some other location in the building. You may or may not get a job offer on the spot. It is common to be asked if you have any other offers or interviews. At most job fairs, once you are offered a job, the school cannot offer it anyone else for 24 hours. It would not be unusual to ask how long you have to decide if the interviewer does not give you that information.

As people accept jobs, the number of openings and positions will decrease. Interviews take place over the second and third day. By the middle of the third day, the pace slows. At the end of the conference, a gala or reception is held for newly hired teachers to meet and socialize with their administrators as a group. Photos will be taken and many people will celebrate through the night. The last day, very little will happen in regard to hiring although administrators might have breakfast with new teachers. For some fairs, this all happens in one day. Everyone leaves and life returns back to normal.

It's stressful, both for administrators and teachers. There are many things you can do to make sure you get noticed and have success. Remember to keep your options open. Most people do not end up with their ideal job on the first try. In fact, positions can change all the time. On the plane headed to my first fair, I ranked my top 10 job choices but by the time the short interviews started on the second morning, all 10 were not listed! I had to start from scratch. If you're only willing to work at one school, then go another route than job fairs. What follows is a list of tips and ideas to secure a job.

Get to the conference early on the first day. It is important to be settled early. You never know who you will meet in the lobby.

Have copies of your CV, resume, reference letters, and reference contacts ready to give a potential employer at a moment's notice. Carry this with you at all times.

Carry business cards that have your contact information and current position. You can get about 200 business cards for $10. This is a solid investment.

Create a one-page (front and back) resume with your photo at the top and references on the other side. Note that you have a longer CV or resume available. Be ready to give a potential administrator your short resume and a business card with details on how they can contact you. The photo is important because the administrator may get twenty or thirty resumes in a few hours.

Dress professionally. You will not get a job dressed in jeans! Most people will be in suits and dresses.

Keep your options open. Do not get dejected that a job has been filled. There are plenty of jobs out there and a poor attitude can be a deal breaker.

Stay at the hotel. Write your room's extension on your business card when you give it to administrators.

Get a cell phone. If you are coming from overseas, it is worth it to buy a cheap phone so people can contact you at any time. A $30 investment in a cell phone could be all it takes to make the difference.

Ask your references to be available. Let them know what you are doing and tell them to expect a call on Saturday morning from an unknown number. It would be a shame to not get a job because a reference did not answer his or her phone.

The changing nature of overseas school employment. The job fair model started many years ago and will probably continue for many years. However, hiring for overseas positions is changing. The advances in communication via the Internet have made interviews via Skype or by telephone much more practical. Sending documents via email is more or less instant. A lot of hiring happens through word of mouth today, especially among teachers with overseas experience. In fact, a lot of hiring happens outside fairs and earlier in the year. Whether this is good or bad, this trend will continue as technology and Internet connections improve. As a new teacher, there is not too much you can do other than look up individual school job pages, email schools in advance, and attend job fairs. The more diligent you are the better your chances of success.

Extra Credit: Although it may be cheaper to stay somewhere else, staying at the hotel makes it much easier for a potential employer to contact you throughout the conference, especially if you are coming from overseas and do not have a cell phone. While I don't think this was the reason I did not get a job at my only fair, I still think it was a mistake on my part.

Recruiting Services

The following list includes some of the most popular recruiting services for overseas teachers. Many regional associations also have job fairs in conjunction with their annual conferences. The job fairs listed below will have hundreds of positions at each fair although the openings decrease as the school year wraps up. As you will see, at least 7,000 positions are filled each year through the major hiring agencies. There is a job waiting for you!

Search Associates. Founded by a former director of an overseas school, Search Associates is bit different than other fairs. Each applicant is screened and has a specific associate assigned to him. The twelve job fairs around the world are by invitation only. They usually begin in November and continue through June, and are held in places like Bangkok, London, Dubai, and Toronto. The application process is thorough but worth it. Search Associates costs $200 for a three-year membership or until you get your first job. In the 2014-2015 they set a record by securing 3,142 overseas positions. This is almost a thousand more than they placed in 2011. The first fair is free and others are $50. The school that recruits you pays a fee for the service. (http://www.searchassociates.com/)

International Schools Services. Known as ISS, this non-profit organization offers schools a variety of services, including teacher recruitment. Like Search, ISS has a detailed application process. Past job fairs have been in Nice, Atlanta, Bangkok, and San Francisco. Its website indicates it has paired over 40,000 candidates and 300 schools over the past 60 years; however, they do not publish the specific number of candidates that accept jobs through their service. (www.iss.edu)

University of Northern Iowa. This is a unique fair which attracts about 1,000 teaching and administration positions worldwide. The fair is in Waterloo, Iowa each February. According to its website, the fair had 596 candidates for 960 positions in 2015 with an average of five interviews. Ninety-five percent of those who received jobs were single without children or teaching couples. The fair costs $150 for individuals and $270 for teaching couples. (www.uni.edu/placement/overseas/)

The International Educator. Known in education circles as TIE, this service is online only. Many schools use this service to complement the different job fairs available. In fact, the FAQ section of their website suggests you use TIe in conjunction with a fair. You can search for jobs by position, location, and other factors and send the school a notification that you are interested. In turn, prospective schools can contact you and you can be notified when a job in your job field opens. TIE currently costs $39 per year, plus $29 if you want the "instant job notification" emails. (www.tieonline.com/)

Extra Credit: If you are at this point in the book, I'd go ahead and sign up with TIE right now. If you are experienced and think you have a pretty good shot of getting a job based on what you've read so far, I'd sign up for the Boston fair with Search Associates. Their process is pretty stringent, but also puts you at a fair with a huge variety of schools. It is also one the first major fairs in the U.S. so there will be more positions available.

Other Methods of Finding Positions

School pages. All overseas schools worth their weight have a good website. This is probably the first point of contact for prospective students. Most websites have a link to job openings. As well, they provide specific information regarding what to send. For example, some ask for a cover letter and CV while others asks for more. If you want certain schools or locations, periodically checking websites is a great idea. It can be laborious but an advantage is that school websites might have the most current information. Schools are more apt to post and update their websites before doing so on the various job-seeking sites. Another advantage is that you are one link closer to the person making the hiring decisions.

Word of mouth. If you know educators who are already teaching overseas, by all means use them. Current overseas teachers will attend conferences, meetings, and other events where they might pick up information before the general public. They are also able to give advice and put in a good word on your behalf. In my experience, this has been valuable to the point that I probably landed one of my jobs through the efforts of a few unsolicited references from overseas teachers.

The local expat. Many teachers are spouses of expatriates working for NGOs, governments, missionaries, and a host of other positions. Others are spouses of host country nationals who have permanently moved to the country. In any case, most schools are eager to hire these qualified teachers for several reasons. Local expat teachers are generally going to be around for many years and will not cost the school a lot in housing and other benefits provided to expatriate foreign hires. As well, they provide continuity between revolving teachers that stay only a few years. Finally, they are generally more eager to 'tow the company line' as they want to keep their jobs for a long time. In my experience, many of these teachers have been excellent in some areas of the school but can also be a bit stagnant in their pedagogy and reluctant to change.

If you are a local expat looking for a job there are ways to improve your chances. You should make yourself known to the school as soon as you are available. School administrators like to know you are in town even if they do not have a position. If the unforeseeable happens with another teacher, they are likely to give you a call on short notice. This happens more often than one would think. At one of my schools, three of about 20 expatriate teachers had to leave for the rest of the school year due to medical reasons. The school hired local expats to fill the gaps.

Although you may be a foreigner, you will most likely be employed as a local. This can get a bit sticky. Being hired as a local may mean you are hired on a local rather than foreign hiring scale and do not receive any of the benefits associated with being a foreigner. Fortunately, many schools are moving to one salary scale for all teachers rather than a local and foreign hiring scale. In the eyes of the school, fiscally they see you as a local and presume your spouse's benefits will cover you as well. Although this is not always the case, this is almost always the result. The section on negotiating may give you some ideas on how to handle this properly before signing a contract.

My Personal Experiences

Finding the right job begins by finding the right places to find an overseas position. Some of the options include word-of-mouth, looking at individual school websites, using online services, and attending fairs. They all have positive and negative aspects. Word-of-mouth and looking at individual school websites are free but can prove difficult for someone with little or no overseas school experience. It is also time consuming. Online-only services are better in the sense that they are relatively inexpensive and put you in direct contact with schools that have positions available. On the other hand, there are many applicants for each position so getting any meaningful response without overseas experience could be an issue. Attending fairs ensures that you will be in direct contact with someone who can offer you a job. Unfortunately, you may spend thousands of dollars along the way on expenses like airfare and hotels.

My experience has changed dramatically from the start of my overseas career until now. I began by interviewing with a school in Nicaragua when I was serving in the Peace Corps. This is an unusual way to get a job unless you are already in the country. My next attempt involved using one of the job fairs in the United States. I came away empty handed and a little dejected. From there, I secured my second job using one of the online services. For my last several jobs, I have directly contacted the schools knowing that I would be moving to the country because of my wife's job. In two cases, I did not get a job initially but secured one after arrival. Fortunately my last two jobs I have secured a contract before moving.

Moving overseas is a gamble. In my opinion, your best bet is to attend a job fair in the United States as early in the season as possible. All of the recruiting firms have different advantages and disadvantages that you will have to weigh before picking one. You will probably spend at least $1,000 and miss at least one or two days of work to have a 60 percent chance of getting a job. Your chances improve greatly if you are relatively young and single, a teaching couple without children, you have an advanced degree, and you have a few years experience. If you have four children, little experience, and a non-teaching spouse, finding a position will prove more difficult. All these factors need to be considered before making the leap.

Salary

Describing overseas salaries and benefits is like trying to describe the salaries and benefits of every district in the United States. While there are some general tendencies, it is nearly impossible to encompass any one school or predict the salary and benefits you will receive. My best advice is to read the contract, ask questions, research and ask others in international education, and decide whether you can live with it or not. For the most part, schools are ethical regarding contracts, work conditions, and just about everything else. However, you occasionally hear horror stories of teachers not getting paid, forcefully being pushed out a country, or even having their passport locked up. Usually there are two sides to the story.

Most schools have standard contracts that are templates for all teachers. You will enter the school at a certain level and step. Each year, the school may be contractually liable for moving you up a step. If you have advanced degrees this will be reflected in the pay scale either through different scales for each type of degree or a base salary with points for each degree. Finally, most schools will account for your experience, although most will only allow around to seven to 10 years of experience regardless of your number of years teaching. If a school does not have a salary scale or adjust salaries for years of experience or degrees, then you have to negotiate a salary. The appendix has an example of a contract that might be a useful starting point.

Base salary. As noted, most schools have a base salary that is a starting point for your income each year. The salary scale adjusts for experience and graduate degrees. If the school has a scale, there is not much negotiating to do. They will simply offer you a position and show you the salary scale and what you will make. You can either agree or decide not to sign the contract. These salary scales are usually developed over time under the direction of the board but may be antiquated. Some teachers like the salary scale while others think it does not reward exemplary service, expertise, and results. From an administrative perspective, a salary scale allows the school to project the budget in future years, it is easy to use, and levels the playing field. Some schools have separate scales for local and foreign staff. Many trailing spouses are given a contract based on the local scale.

If you must negotiate it is important to meticulously review the materials in this book and other resources for different components that you want in your contract. For example, besides negotiating your base salary it is important to factor in the other benefits. The section below goes into much more detail about benefits. Depending on location and the cost of living, you could start with your current salary and move from there. For example, if you make $50,000 in a suburb of Chicago and you are moving to an expensive city in Europe you might expect the base salary to increase. In turn, a rural school in South America may pay you much less. Keep in mind that saving potential is just as important as your actual salary.

How you get paid is another important factor. Some schools will pay you in U.S. dollars, others in the local currency, and some will offer you a choice. Most people, if given the choice, get paid mostly in U.S. dollars and take a small percentage in the local currency to cover monthly expenses in the host country. In places where the currency is stronger than the U.S. dollar, many teachers prefer to get paid in the local currency and transfer money to their U.S. bank account.

Other ways to enhance income. There are many ways to enhance your income. It really boils down to the contract, your free time, and your will to make more money. Some places have opportunities at school while others have none. Common income supplements include a retirement allowance, cost-of-living allowance, coaching, clubs or extended trips, tutoring, and teaching outside school.

Many schools offer a retirement plan. As noted in the financial section, very few schools today have an in-house retirement plan. Instead they usually give you a small percentage of your base salary to invest in your retirement. In some cases, you are free to do what you want with the money. Some people invest all of it into a retirement plans while others consider the money part of their income.

Another source of income in many schools is a cost-of-living allowance. This is factored into many contracts, especially those in Europe, as a way to guard against fluctuations in inflation and provide teachers with an adjusted income each year. This is usually done on a yearly basis and is factored with overall inflation rates. Here is a quick example. A teacher receives a base salary of $50,000. If the cost of living in the first year of the contract is 2.3 percent, that would bring the total income to $51,150. The next year, prices increase dramatically and the teacher gets 3.8 percent. That would bring the total income to $51,900. The board often sets these rates after taking into account inflation and the school's financial situation. Every so often the base salary is increased to reflect the overall gradual inflation.

Almost all coaching and other extracurricular activities are either a requirement in your contract or include a stipend. If they are included in your contract, you will usually be asked to cover at least one quarter, trimester, or season. This could be as a coach, mentor, advisor, director, or anything else. These will probably not be paid if they are written into your contract. In other schools, teachers will be asked if they can coach or advise anything. This often happens in their interview. This should not be taken lightly as it could make the difference between getting a position or not. If you do coach or lead an activity, you will be expected to travel with the team. In return, you will receive a small stipend around $500 to $1,000. Some might not consider this a benefit while others enjoy it and like the free travel.

Other teachers supplement their income through clubs and trips with students but outside the purview of the school. This may include a winter ski trip, a trip organized to visit Europe over spring break, a summer camp focusing on technology, and just about anything else. In my experiences, these types of clubs and trips follow the same pattern. An established, long-serving teacher in the school hosts some type of event, camp, or trip with the blessing of the administration or board. Over time, these activities either expand or fall apart. If they succeed, the established teacher will ask other teachers if they want to help out in exchange for a small stipend or a free trip.

Tutoring, especially in English or math, can be lucrative. Some schools have established tutoring programs that allow teachers to tutor a small group of students during set hours each week. Others are more lax. Teachers might tutor a few students once or twice a week for an hour after school. This can be a great way to earn extra income as the pay is usually immediate and worth the time if you have it. Schools should have policies on tutoring. For example, some schools may exclude teachers from tutoring altogether while others exclude teachers from tutoring their own students. In any case, make sure you clear this with your administration before taking on a student.

One of the last ways to make money is on the local market. You may be able to find local work but it will depend on what type of visa you have, work agreements between the host country and the United States, and school policy. This might include teaching English on Saturday mornings, running a youth group, or working with music in some capacity. Every country is different and so are the opportunities. With a little research most people could supplement their income if the school allows it. This may not be a good idea in your first year of a new school. You may want to spend time learning the school policies and your curriculum.

Let's go through a quick example of potential income. A teacher signs a contract for $50,000 with a ten percent retirement supplement. The cost of living allowance is 4.2 percent because the base salaries (on the salary scale) have not been adjusted in several years. The teacher coaches two sports throughout the year and tutors a student twice a week ($35 per hour) in the morning for another $3,000. The teacher's actual income including retirement would be $60,100. This income would be free of federal taxes in most cases as the U.S. federal government does not take taxes from an individual if the overall income is below $100,800 (2015). In addition, the teacher probably visited two other countries while coaching. Depending on other benefits such as free housing and a flight back home each year, this person could save a good portion of his or her salary while living well. If they are a trailing spouse, like me, or a teaching couple, a large portion of the salary could be saved. I have been able to save more than seventy-five percent of my salary for the last four years although this is quite unusual.

Extra Credit: Some schools have some wiggle room, if they really want you. Some schools might be able to hire you at a step or two higher than your experience. If you are pretty confident, or in a position where the school really needs you, it is worth asking for more money or benefits.

Benefits

If your salary represents the meat and potatoes of overseas education, the benefits represent the dessert. The first tier of benefits should be included in your package; if they are not, you should consider whether this is the school for you. The second tier of benefits could be compared to a second helping of dessert. If you get any of these, you are in good shape. Finally, there are some benefits that are rarely found in contracts. These might indicate the school is in a great financial situation and wants to hire the best teachers available. These schools are willing to go the extra mile to get the best of the best. On the other hand, some schools have trouble filling contracts or have high teacher attrition.

Usually found in packages. Most contracts include standard items. These benefits would carry over to your spouse and dependents are well. Almost all contracts cover travel to and from the school at the beginning and end of your contract. Schools also provide help and expenses for visas and other paperwork. They help in this regard so you can work. Most schools offer some type of group medical coverage, although you may have to pay a deductible and monthly assessment. Schools will require teachers to participate in extracurricular activities, although this may be paid. Many schools offer some type of retirement benefit. Finally, and most importantly for some, schools provide tuition for your dependents. There might be limits to the number of children and it may not include children under three years old. If your school does not provide any of the benefits listed above, you should ask about them because they are expensive.

Found in most packages. Although it is more standard in some parts of the world, schools in many places give you a housing allowance. In some cases, this will not cover all your housing expenses and is available for a limited number of years. Schools use this as a method of reducing the costs associated with teachers who have been at the school a long time and drain the school's budget. Another excellent perk is providing flights back to your home of record every year for you and your family. Some schools only offer this at the beginning and end of your contract. Other schools offer some type of dental plan. Schools generally offer to pick up some portion of your electricity, water, gas, Internet or other monthly expenses. Finally, many schools have funds set aside for the death of immediate family members back in the United States.

Rarely found in packages. There are some benefits that are not very common. Although some schools provide full housing, this is unusual. Providing an allowance that covers some or most of the rent is more common. The exception would be schools that have on-campus housing or a housing compound where all the teachers live. Still other schools provide cars to incoming teachers. This is an excellent benefit as it provides transportation without the hassle of trying to get your car fixed when it breaks and you probably won't need to pay for insurance. Many schools have special benefits that might not be available in other locations. For example, in one of my schools we were allowed commissary privileges, a benefit usually reserved only for the diplomatic community.

Most of these benefits apply to the entire teaching faculty and probably can't be changed without the school board changing the policy. In other words, you probably will not be able to negotiate a housing allowance if it is not a part of the benefits package. In the six schools I have taught in so far, four provided full housing, one provided a stipend which covered about eighty percent of expenses, and one offered none. Two schools offered a plane ticket back to your country of record each year.

Professional Qualifications

Licensure. If you are already a teacher, it is a good idea to get your license renewed or updated before moving. Most schools will require it as part of the contract. After that, many teachers will forget about it until they move to the next school. Teachers who stay in one school a long time often forget to get it renewed or simply not do it. I would strongly suggest you keep it updated. There is always the chance that your school will require you to show it to them on short notice, regardless of how long you have been there. One day in Vienna the administration received word from the Austrian government that they needed to see the professional qualifications for all their teachers. While everyone at the school had a license, some teachers had to scramble to get them renewed or updated.

Undergraduate vs. Master's Degree. Many overseas teachers have a Master's degree. Many job descriptions require a Master's degree and will not consider applicants without one. This is a way schools can be selective and ensure that most applicants will have at least a few years of experience. There are many online university programs and even some that specialize in overseas education. If you do not have one, I would suggest you consider this before telling your current principal you are not coming back next year because you want to teach overseas. It is not a deal breaker in some schools, but of all the items that principals look at, this is important. I was initially hired without a Master's, but I was living in the country, spoke the language, and agreed to be hired as a local. They likely would not have considered me had I contacted them from the States. One last thing to consider is where you want to work. There are many schools in less-desirable locations that will hire someone without a Master's.

Experience overseas. You either have experience teaching overseas or you don't. Hopefully, if you don't, you at least have a few years of good experience. Of the hundreds of teachers I have taught with in overseas schools on four continents, I can only think of one that was a first-year teacher. Teaching overseas (or living overseas for extended periods of time and having teaching experience) is the most important factor in getting a job overseas. Schools spend a lot of time, money, and resources hiring new teachers and they do not want teachers who are going to leave after the first semester. A proven record of living or teaching overseas is a big deal. It shows that you will probably not leave and cause havoc at the school. If you have lived overseas you are at an advantage over those who have not, so highlight your experience on your resume or CV. Even mention an exchange program in high school but stick away from indicating you spent four spring breaks in Cancun.

Experience is another important consideration. Even if you do not have much overseas experience, your work in U.S. schools is important. The more years you have, the better your chances of getting a job that would be considered top tier. It seems many young teachers without a lot of experience teach in less-desirable locations or those that pay less.

After a few years, the door is open to many more possibilities. Do not overlook these positions. You can often save money and continue your education while working overseas. For example, although I had three years of teaching in the United States before starting my overseas career, I would probably not have gotten at least two or three jobs _ Rabat, Vienna, and Dakar _ because they most likely screen out teachers who have no overseas experience. If you are considering staying overseas you may think of your first job as a stepping stone to getting to your ideal location. Keep in mind, most overseas teachers end up at several schools.

IB and AP experience. Many schools around the world have IB and AP classes. Although the AP program is offered only for high school, the IB program begins with elementary school. If you have taught in an IB or AP school, you have an advantage. If you have taken any training in IB or AP, you are at an advantage. Like a Master's degree, many schools will only hire people with IB or AP experience. If you do not have any, there are a few options. First, you could consider transferring to a school in your district that offers IB or AP. If that is not realistic, both IB and AP have extensive training for teachers. When hired for my first job at both an IB school and AP school, I was offered and accepted trainings in the United States over the summer. It was really helpful.

Extracurricular activities. There is really no downside for having any extracurricular activity experience. Even if a school does not offer what you have experience with, it shows that you are a team player, passionate about children, and willing to go the extra mile. As crazy as it sounds, some schools hire people based on their ability to fill in coaching or extracurricular activities. In some schools, the talent pool might be small and the need for someone to direct the play might supersede other attributes. I am sure of one person who got a job because she was the only person interviewed who was willing to fill a volleyball position.

Leadership. Keep in mind that almost all overseas schools are single entities without a central office. As such, many teachers not only teach but direct curricula, head committees, and do a host of leadership activities. Any leadership you can offer to the school is an advantage. Some teachers get hired for their leadership experience. Becoming a team leader, heading up the calendar committee, or doing anything that shows leadership could give you an advantage over other applicants.

Training. Any training you have had is important. Although training in the subjects or grade level that you will be teaching are better, be sure to include everything. The more professional development you have had translates to better classroom teaching. I cannot think of any downside to getting or including training as part of your experience.

Interviewing

Interviewing for an overseas teaching job is similar to any interviewing. It is a short, high-stakes session that determines your future. The more prepared you are the better off you will be. Although people can be coached to interview well, this section will only cover the nuances that might be different from non-overseas schools. Before going to a fair or talking to a potential principal, it is super important to practice and be ready for their questions. There are a lot websites and resources available to help. The appendix contains a list of questions you may be asked that are directly related to working and teaching overseas.

Email etiquette. An email to the principal will probably be your first contact. Obviously, someone should proofread everything before sending it. Keep your first contact as simple as possible with no more than a few attachments.

The content of the email should be simple. In the subject line include the position you are interested in. Find out if the principal is male or female and address them with any title such Dr. as needed.

Include a short paragraph explaining why you are interested. Include a few lines or bullet points that highlight your qualifications and experience. Try to include something that indicates you know specifics about the school. Finish with a reference to your resume/CV and cover letter as attachment and ask if they would be interested in you contacting them if you have a question or want further information. This reverts from asking a question to telling them you will contact them. The appendix includes a sample resume/CV and cover letter. In short, make the initial contact short and professional. There is no need to show them your creativity by using some artistic font. If you have a good website, a link to it is a good idea. If your website is antiquated and not used much, disregard it for now.

Phone etiquette. If you've made it to the phone interview you can assume the school is interested. A phone interview is an effective way for the school to learn if what they have seen via email and documents translates to you personally. They also want to know about your personal life, goals, ideas, and lifestyle. In my experience, I have had this phone call several times. In one instance, we spent approximately 80 percent of the time talking about my teaching experiences. In another interview, I was only asked a few questions about teaching and spent the majority of the call talking about things my hobbies, interests, family life; all subjects unrelated to school. The first interviewer wanted to find out if I would be a good teacher, the second interviewer wanted to see if I would fit into the school.

Be prepared for a phone interview. The interview time will probably be scheduled with the principal in mind. Be ready to wake up at 3:30 a.m. for a 4 a.m. interview.

My interview for my latest job in Dakar involved driving from a campground in Pennsylvania to a McDonald's in the nearest town. Not only did the principal see me on the computer screen but he also saw a painting of Ronald McDonald. I used the unusual situation as an introduction and I got the job.

Have as many resources around you as possible. At a minimum, have your resume/CV and brief answers to the most-likely questions. Some people suggest dressing as you would for a face-to-face interview. It might increase your confidence. Personally, I always wear my favorite pullover, as it is the thing I feel the most comfortable in.

Know the school. Before the interview you should click through the school's website. If there is not that much, write some questions that you want answered. Some advisors believe that if you don't have any questions, it's a sign you do not really care. Also, take a few minutes to look at the city and country. A few words describing how you looked at some day trips will go a long way in showing you are really interested. If the school has programs that you are unfamiliar with it would be a good idea to take a quick look at those websites, too. Think in terms of them hiring the most qualified person for the job. Certainly, other applicants will know or have experience in some areas of the school's program. If you do not know anything about it, your chances of getting the position diminish.

Videoconference etiquette. At a recent roundtable of middle school principals, I learned a few observations about video conferencing using Skype or something similar. They cited poorly dressed teachers who continually forgot they were on camera. The biggest problems they identified were poor dress, not looking at the camera, and reading scripted responses directly from their computer. Follow the same strategies you would for a phone interview. A few examples of student work sitting next to you can be used as examples in the same way you might show a portfolio piece. Although I have never done this, you can also send documents during the interview as needed. Finally, it is fine to have some notes or ideas written on the wall in front of you. Use them like a teleprompter to get ideas for responses. The more organized you are, the better off you will be.

In person. In-person interviews are excellent opportunities for you to show yourself to your future principal. Obviously, dress the part. With little exception, you should be wearing a suit, dress or something very nice. Remember, this is for a teaching job, just in a different location. Have an extra copy of your resume, general cover letter, reference list, and business cards available. Many people will have a portfolio, as well.

Contracts

Basic components. No need to beat a dead horse, but a professional overseas contract should have certain components in it. Keep in mind that these schools are independent entities, national laws may supersede school desires, and contracts are legally binding documents so the language may be somewhat different than what you were told in your interview. The appendix includes an example of a typical contract. A good contract includes information regarding your professional duties as a teacher, your responsibilities outside the classroom, and the benefits you will receive.

Things to look for in a contract. There are several things that might be considered red flags in a contract. For the most part, anything that is not included in your contract is generally not binding while everything in it is binding. Discrepancies between the interview and contract should not be taken lightly. For example, if you are told that you will be given round-trip airfare at the beginning and end of your contract, make sure it is in print. If not, either do not sign it or consider the possibility that you will pay your own airfare. Any school worth joining will include these types of benefits in their contracts. This goes for everything that you talk about or negotiate in your contract.

Other things that should be addressed in your contract are your number of classes, hours of contact time in a week, contact days, housing benefits, insurance, and retirement. If you agreed verbally to these items and they are not in the contract, get clarification in writing before signing. Besides specific items, you want to make sure the contract is professional. Just like questions in a survey should be specific, so should each component of the contract. Any vague wording or anything that is not clear should be talked about after having a chance to review the contract.

Finances and taxes are another concern. Some schools are scrupulous about your exact salary, local taxes, and local retirement taxes. Be sure to get exact numbers on all of these in order to make an assessment of how much money you will be able to take home. A large initial salary might be cut by twenty to thirty percent due to local taxes and a local retirement fund that will not benefit you.

There should be a timeframe for deciding on a contract. Do not get intimidated if the person interviewing you asks for a signature on the spot. Tell the person you want a little bit of time to read the document, reflect, and ask questions as needed. You also might have other interviews or contract offers on the table. It is less likely you will run into this problem in more established schools around the world that have clear procedures, standard benefits, and a salary scale. Reading some of the overseas schools websites and blogs, it appears the proliferation of proprietary schools has caused some problems for a small but important group of teachers.

Negotiating. Books are written about this topic. I am sure of this because I remember one sitting on my dad's reading shelf growing up. Unfortunately, I never read it, but I have heard enough from other teachers to know that in some schools, negotiating is possible. If a school really wants or needs you, there is a good chance there is somewhere in the contract that you can negotiate. This might be a couple of steps up on the salary scale, a larger moving allowance for your family, or 100 other ways.

While it is never wrong to ask about a bit of wiggle room or something to entice you to come to a school, this should be done with humility. Many overseas schools are nonprofit organizations that do not have millions of dollars tucked away in a foreign bank account waiting for you (and your spouse) to tap. In fact, some schools may be stretched thin and cannot offer you anything more than a standard package given to all teachers. Some things that are really worth considering before you decide to negotiate are your level of interest in the school, the amount you would need to go there, other acceptable offers on the table, and the number of people interviewing for the same position. If there were no chance you would go to the school unless they increase their offer, then it is probably not worth your while. However, if a few thousand dollars more in savings would make the difference, it is definitely worth trying. Just like every other job, if the employer really wants you, they will do what it takes to make sure you sign a contract.

The whole idea of negotiating relies on supply and demand. The larger the pool of teachers willing to sign a contract, the less likely a school would be to negotiate. With that being said, more established schools in big cities will probably be much less likely to negotiate anything whereas a small school in the middle of nowhere might be more willing. Although I do not know this as fact, I would assume the company-owned schools would be more likely to negotiate contracts on an individual basis like they would an executive. Finally, almost all schools will be somewhat familiar with this system as most administration positions are negotiated individually.

How to find out about a school once you have an offer.
Congratulations on getting offered a job! Now what? Well, unless you accept the offer on the spot and this is the school you are 100 percent sure you want to be at for the next few years, a little more research is warranted. Of course, you want to examine the school's website. Look for specific documents like board meeting minutes, policies, and any handbooks for teachers, parents or students. Talk to contacts that might know about the school. Finally, you could go to websites that rate schools and administrators. This last option should be taken with a grain of salt as many of the postings are not vetted or fact checked. Finally, the U.S. Department of State supports approximately 200 schools around the world. If your school is supported, the department's Office of Overseas Schools may be able to provide some information.

Accepting a job. Hopefully you will be able to accept a job in person. If you are at a conference, some administrators will ask you to make a decision quickly so they can offer the job to someone else at the same conference (provided you decline). This is more apt to happen as the hiring season winds down or with schools that are not attending many fairs. Some schools with large faculties or lots of hiring each year may go to five or six conferences while others will attend just one.

At most conferences, once a job is offered you should have 24 hours before the job can be offered to someone else. If you already have an offer, don't be afraid to use it as leverage. Friends of mine got a $10,000 increase to their joint salary by telling the school they couldn't accept the job because another school had offered $10,000 more. Somehow the school found a way to hire them by adjusting some numbers and years of experience.

If you are unable to respond in person, a phone call is the best route to take. Even if you decline, it is best to call the person and deliver the message formally. As a last resort, email the principal or director and let them know your decision. Obviously, due to travel, time changes, or other factors, the person who offered you the job may ask that you respond via email.

Declining a job. Many people come out of job fairs with several offers. For example, if you and your wife have fifteen years of IB experience in science and math, you will probably have more than one offer at a conference. (In reality, you will probably not even need to go to a conference and might need to make you phone number unlisted). Anyway, if you have more than one offer, it is only proper to tell the person who made the offer in a timely manner. I would suggest waiting until you have signed another contract and ensuring that everything you negotiated about over the interview is in the contract you want to sign. After that, a quick phone call or personal visit with the person who offered you the job would be acceptable. There is no need to be overly dramatic or give a 10-minute soliloquy, simply tell the person that after careful reflection you decided to go to __ School. Keep in mind that they do this several times each year and will probably not be offended. They might even sweeten their offer if you have not signed the other contract. Although not very common, I have heard of this happening. In any case, be sure to thank them for the opportunity, wish them luck in finding someone for the position, and say that you hope to work together in the future.

If you have left the conference, had a video or phone interview, or cannot find the person who offered you the job, the protocol depends on the situation. Really, just like in person, you should tell the person as soon as possible after you have either signed a contract or are 100 percent sure you do not want to go to that school. Unless you see the person on Skype, there is no need to wait to tell the person in a 'live' format; an email or phone call should suffice. Again, you do not need to write 1,000 words explaining why you chose to go to another school. A simple, one-paragraph email with your decision is all that is needed. Thank the person for their time and if you liked the person, say that you hope it might work out in the future.

8 Between hiring and moving- a long process

Now that you have been hired, what do you do? In a nutshell, you must store or sell most of your belongings, say goodbye to friends and family, and prepare to move. This chapter will briefly describe a generic timeline, what to bring, preparing your home and preparing your family and friends.

Timeline

Many new teachers are hired in January and February. This gives you roughly six or seven months to get everything together. In the first few weeks, you will probably spend time learning about the school and country while letting your friends and family know that you are moving overseas. This is an exciting period as you have decided to make a huge change in your life. Almost everything will be positive as you learn more about the best places to visit, the culture, as well as some introductory material from the school such as the orientation schedule and contact information from the person you are replacing.

If you are like many teachers, the next couple of months will focus on finishing your requirements at the school you are leaving. Your focus will be more on the current school and not too much will happen regarding the new school. You might exchange emails with other incoming teachers and receive a few emails from the school. As the school year winds down you will need to start thinking about what you must do before leaving. There are two main things to do: decide what you will bring, and sell or store everything else.

The last month or so will include a flurry of activity. You will spend night after night saying goodbye to friends and family. You might pack, unpack, and pack your suitcase over and over again until the zippers wear out. I am guilty of this. During this time you will also get your plane tickets, hopefully from the school, and get ready to go.

What to Bring

Bringing the right items to your post is important. There are a couple of ways to think about this. A lot depends on any shipping allowance, your personal tastes, and the number of people moving with you. Most people are given a small allowance for shipping that will not cover all expenses. Many schools offer between $1,000 and $2,000. Others bring extra suitcases on their flight and absorb the cost. Still others buy what they need on the local economy. At one of my posts, I moved with two suitcases. I was single. Two of my fellow new teachers, both with families of four, shared a full-sized shipping container. In the end, we were all happy. I bought local items like a television and coffee maker with the money I saved on shipping. They spent way more than the school gave them but they had everything they wanted. Now, I have my own family of four. During a recent move, we had approximately 6,000 pounds, excluding furniture. This could be used as a reference before deciding what to keep, what to store, and what to discard.

There are a few things you should include when moving. Clothing for work and leisure is a no-brainer. Overseas educators tend to dress more relaxed than teachers in the States but it is important to have nice clothes. A few people wear suits every day while others wear jeans. A school in an Asian capital is probably more formal than a Caribbean outpost. Your school probably has parameters but you definitely want to bring at least a suit or dress for special occasions. Next, you should hand carry any important documents, prescriptions and electronics in your carry-on bag. These are the items you cannot do without and replacing them would be a nightmare.

Although there is no tried-and-true list, it is important to bring certain items. If you have just two suitcases, I suggest packing them full of work clothes and an electronic or two. If you are taking a few hundred pounds, add some toiletries that you cannot get in the host country (ask someone ahead of time), linens, sporting equipment, more electronics, and a few items to make your new residence feel like home. Once you start moving more than a few hundred pounds, you should begin to set limits. Scale back on things you have not worn in several years, you probably won't wear them in a foreign country, either. Even if I knew I was moving to a country for several years, I would think hard about each piece of furniture. If I love it, I might bring it. If I just like it, I would store or toss it. Smaller, lightweight items make more sense because many shipping companies charge by weight.

Teacher Time: Moving to the developing world.... by Lawrence E.

Admittedly, as a father, the notion of bringing my wife and tweenaged son, to Khartoum was both exciting and daunting, but all apprehensions dissipated within the first 48 hours of our arrival.

The fully equipped quarters assigned to us is quite pleasant, maintaining the yard is a task we assigned to our son, who is thrilled that (finally) he is designated with household responsibility. Of course, making the house a home comes from within one's perception; it took a couple of weeks to settle in, rearranging furniture and such. We sampled most of the food of the surrounding restaurants but I knew, the night my son and I came home to the mixed aromas of my wife Annette's kitchen; home baked bread, steamed rice and adobo; we were home.

Working in KICS is a pleasure, the environment is one that is inspiring, what with helpful staff and eager students. Though work may be challenging, again it is a matter of attitude, I enjoy what I do, teaching… educating young minds.

Bringing a tween to Khartoum was one of the worries we mulled upon, what was there for him to do? There are no cinemas or play arenas. There aren't many options, but surprisingly he has adjusted very well. He has enjoyed the play dates and birthday parties he has attended, where he has actually PLAYED outdoors and had conversations with friends.

My family enjoys exploring whatever country we are in. Annette has always been interested in Egyptian and Nubian history, seeing the Nubian pyramids was a thrill I had to grant her. We look forward to more road trips in this fascinating country.

Most of every basic necessity is available in Khartoum, even if they are relatively pricey. But like most international workers know, we should bring what we might not need, but must have, when we do need it. Basic medicines, fill out your prescriptions (if any) abroad, preferred toiletry brands and the like. You may want to consider bringing what you deem as a basic appliance in your home country, being Asians, we brought a rice cooker and a bread maker.

All told, living in Sudan could be testing, but like I said, it depends on one's mind-set. We do what the locals do, we have tea by the Nile, enjoy the museum, we sample the myriad of international food that is available everywhere, and we do everything as a family. **Keep an open mind and welcome the experience**

> *Lawrence E. is a drama teacher at the Khartoum International Community School in Khartoum, Sudan.*

Pets

Although bringing a pet may be high on your list of priorities, it can be a time-consuming and expensive ordeal. However, if you have the motivation it can be done. My family has successfully moved with our family dog four times. In the process, we have spent thousands of dollars and had several bureaucratic hurdles to clear. My wife and daughter would say this has been worth it.

Here are the basic steps needed to transport a pet. First, the time of year is important. Most airlines in the United States will not transport dogs during the summer or if the temperature is above a certain level on the day of departure. This can be an issue when returning to the States for the summer, as well. Airline restrictions vary, but generally if your pet is under fifteen pounds and has enough room to sit up and turn around inside his or her container, then you can transport the pet in the passenger cabin. If not, the pet must be transferred as cargo or extra baggage. Meanwhile, some airlines prohibit all pets from the cabin, regardless of size. Exceptions are usually made for service pets.

Make sure the country you are moving to allows pets to enter. For example, one country might have a quarantine period of up to six months while another requires an electronic chip and vaccinations within a certain time period. Other considerations include purchasing an FAA-approved crate, paying for someone to care for your pet during transition, and getting the paperwork together well in advance. Most countries require a rabies vaccination. Invariably you will need to make at least one trip to the veterinarian's office. Once at your new home there will probably be a veterinarian that most teachers use.

Costs can be out of control. Here is an extreme example. My friends in Madagascar moved from Guatemala. They spent about $5000 getting their dog from Guatemala to Madagascar. It also took several different attempts, a service in Paris, and several months. We have spent up to $1000 getting our dog from one post to another. However, recently, we've been lucky spending our dog as extra baggage for about $200.

Preparing Your Home

Time to have a yard sale? Moving your childhood stuffed animal collection from one part of town to another may now cost you hundreds of dollars to move overseas. Depending on your location in the United States and the location you are moving to, your shipment may be moved via rail, truck, ship, or plane. It is in your best interest to store items that you won't use or need overseas. Many overseas teachers rely on family members to store keepsakes and other important items. Others pay for storage space. Another alternative is to move items to a summer home. All of these have advantages and disadvantages.

I should briefly mention that many teachers have been overseas for many years. A good majority of them thought they would be overseas just a few years before returning back to their normal life. Their adventure has turned into a lifestyle. They end up paying monthly fees for yard sale fodder for many years. Parents start to get upset because those couches that you said would only be there a few years have been in their basement for seventeen years. In a nutshell, keep the stuff you really want and get rid of the rest.

Preparing Family and Friends

If your friends don't think you are crazy, they definitely think you are weird. Why would you ever want to move from the United States? Don't we have everything you could ever want? Are you a Benedict Arnold or what? Being from Kentucky, many of my friends don't even like to cross the Ohio River to go to Indiana. After fourteen years overseas, a handful of my friends think I'm still crazy and don't understand, but most do understand and many have even visited me. I should have better prepared my friends and family for my move overseas, but I did not know how.

Be honest. Tell your friends and family that you are looking for an adventure but still want to be responsible. After years of doing the same thing over and over, you want a challenge. Nothing in the world is that far anymore. (My mom may disagree with this one after we moved to Nepal and Madagascar.) As you learn about the country, share it with people. However, don't be that person who can't talk about anything else. Nobody wants to hear a lecture on Senegal's groundnuts industry. You know your friends and family and can probably figure out how to get them on board. It's better to do this before you leave.

Without being too preachy, a lot of colleagues have had parents or other loved ones die while they are overseas. If you have any grudges with family members or friends, they won't end just because you're moving overseas.

Once you arrive, it is important to keep family and friends informed. Unlike twenty years ago, when the most efficient way to communicate was through the post office, there are many ways to communicate immediately. Many teachers have personal blogs, although this has waned a bit with the advent of social media such as Facebook and Instagram. If you have a decent Internet connection, there are many ways to communicate via audio and video methods. Some of the most popular current options are Skype, Vonage, Face Time, and Magic Jack.

9 THE FIRST YEAR OVERSEAS

So what does it mean to actually live overseas? I can remember the anxiety I felt in the weeks and months before shipping off to the Peace Corps in Nicaragua. Although I knew I wanted to do it, I was unsure of what I was getting myself into. Even though I did not have many specific questions (I had asked all those), I had some lingering doubts. This chapter is split into two parts. The first part explains the stages of living overseas from the first few weeks of excitement to moving back to the United States. The second part is a timeline of the first two years overseas from the day you get off the plane to your second year as an overseas teacher. If you can make it two years, you can probably make it forever!

Stages of Overseas Living

Many have talked about the stages of living abroad. There are five main stages: a honeymoon period, a WTF period, acceptance, assimilation, and repatriation. Each stage can last anywhere between a few days and a few years depending on your personality, the differences between your culture and the one you are assimilating into, and the support you receive. The time periods I provide seem to be the most logical based on my experience and those around me. Inevitably, there will be some extreme highs and lows. As I recall, I was in the honeymoon phase for about six months and then crashed into the WTF period. After your first move to another overseas country, you will likely still experience these periods but to a lesser a degree.

The honeymoon phase is the first few weeks when living in the country might actually feel more like a vacation because of the support you receive. Everything is new and exciting. This usually lasts a few weeks to a month. You will survive on nervous energy and excitement. You will have a lot of support and structure from the school.

The WTF period can last much longer, depending on you and your environment. This is when you look at anything within the school or community and wish it could be like your hometown. For example, you do not understand why the school uses a certain bus system that seems inefficient or you do not understand why the country does not have bleach. You used it all the time back home. Frustration may overtake you in instances and places that never would have happened before. Longing for family, friends, and the comforts of home is normal. This usually lasts from about the first month for a few months to a year.

Eventually, this period turns into acceptance. You realize that the school uses the bus service because it is the best option available. There is no bleach because the country does not have the resources to produce it, or doesn't import it. Traffic, the Internet, and other things that drove you crazy before make more sense. You might even agree with it and at the very least you can accept it. At school, you understand certain policies or procedures that you thought were ridiculous at the beginning of the year. Issues you would have fought for a year ago either seem acceptable or not worth fighting for anymore. The acceptance period may start as early as few months after your arrival to a year or so.

Assimilation is a sign that you are truly a member of the community. People ask you questions about the school and country that you never thought you knew. You can answer questions about the school's history and the politics of the country at length. Those petty little issues that you could not understand a few years back are not even worth talking about now, in fact, you think they are better. Sometimes you do not consort with new teachers because in your mind they tend to be so negative about the country. Chances are you have some good host country friends and your language skills are at least good enough to carry on a conversation with anyone. Bottom line, you like the country and may not consider moving for a long time. Assimilation usually happens after a few years or it might take much longer.

The longer you live overseas the more likely repatriation into your home country will be difficult. Things that you took for granted seem crazy to you now. The opinions of your friends and family may not have changed, but you have. Going back to your country, even for summer visits, may be a mix of euphoria and depression. Some even say repatriation is much harder than assimilating into a new country.

I remember my first visit back to the United States in 2005 after two years in Nicaragua. I remember four things distinctly: neon signs everywhere, people were overweight, everyone was on their cell phones, and it was loud. It took me a few days to get the courage to go to Walmart. Although I still love my family and friends, there are many things I do not understand anymore about the United States. For example, why do most people I know run their air conditioners when the weather is pleasant outside? Some of my friends and family have the same routines they've had for ten or fifteen years. Don't they want a little more excitement in their lives? It's these types of questions I still deal with every time I'm back in the States. At this point, I am not sure I ever want to live in the States permanently, or do I?

Moving Overseas

First day. Your first day in your new home may be one of the most exciting and difficult times of your life. I remember vivid details about my first day overseas. I was with a group of other Peace Corps volunteers and most of us were overwhelmed. Unlike other trips I had taken overseas, this one was different as I was going to live in the country rather than just visit it for a few weeks. I felt like I had to absorb everything. Now picture the same feeling added with meeting your new boss, going to a new school, meeting other new teachers, and possibly having to deal with jet lag, kids, and new accommodations. It can be overwhelming.

I have experienced six schools on four continents and the orientation program provided by the school has generally been the same. The first day, an administrator will meet you at the airport with a van for luggage and your family. You usually go to the school briefly to see it, and then head to your temporary or permanent housing. If you are going to live on the school's compound, you usually go there. Some schools will set up a short-term lease before you arrive. This gives you time to decide if you want the housing provided for you or look for something else. It would not be out of line to ask about your housing before arriving. I am sure some schools do very little while others can be overwhelming. Usually, the rest of the day is free to relax in your new abode and get settled in your surroundings. The school might provide a dinner or some type of entertainment in the evening to get you more settled.

As you arrive, remember that the school is closed, administrators probably just arrived back from their holidays, and not everything will go as smoothly as planned. One teacher I worked with described having to use the curtains from the school's housing the first night because no one at the school provided linens. At another school, I was asked what I liked to eat and I arrived to a refrigerator full of prepared food.

First week. After surviving your first day and getting some rest, the first week will be a whirlwind of activities. Your school will provide some type of orientation, time for planning and setting up your classroom, social engagements during the day and night, and a few practical excursions.

It is very likely your school has an established orientation or welcoming program. This usually happens a few days before returning teachers arrive back at school. In my experience, you will have an opportunity to meet people from the different divisions and areas of the school, a chance to set up your classroom, planning, and other school-related activities. During this week, someone might take all the new teachers to the grocery store, cell-phone depot, and other practical locations. Social activities might include fun team-building activities like a bike ride or visit to local historical sites. At night you most likely will be invited to dinner (as a group) with the head of school and other administrators.

If you have children, the school should help with childcare during the orientation program. This could be as simple as recommending a babysitter to providing in-school childcare. Be sure to ask about this before arriving and ask for help if you need it. The first week should be about orienting yourself to the school and community. Everything you can do to make the transition more palatable for your family and yourself is important. Sorry to be gross, but don't be surprised if you have some stomach issues as well.

First month. In the first month you will get into a daily routine. This will include some routine during school days and another one for the weekends. This will be a period of intense discovery. You will go from always wondering if you are lost to being able to get to the grocery store without thinking about it. Other spots, such as a place to get a haircut, will be confusing but you should be more confident than you were in the first few days. You may or may not feel comfortable taking taxis or public transportation. You will be exhausted from all the activity of school and life outside school.

After the first month, you will have a much better idea of the school. If you work on a team, you will know the other members by now and might even be comfortable speaking in meetings. You will have a much better idea about the student population, culture, school leadership, and policies. Unless you have a lot of overseas experience, this is a good time for listening and observing. Many new teachers in overseas schools come in with ideas from their old school that may not be practical for a variety of reasons.

First six months. By the first six months you will be much more comfortable with the school and your life overseas. This does not necessarily mean you like it, but at least you are comfortable getting through each day. You will know if you made a great decision to move overseas or if the experiment was unsuccessful. You should have a firm idea about the school and community. You no longer spend all your time discovering; you spend your time educating. By this time, you might feel comfortable traveling more freely in the country or region and finding new places to visit. Hopefully, you have people within the community you can rely on for questions and help. One more benefit of living in the country is that you no longer order bread when you meant to order a salad and you know when a taxi is taking you in the right direction. This probably means your host country language skills are at least at the survival level.

First year. By the end of your first year, you will be looking both forward and back. Looking forward, you have a clear idea about the school and your expectations and can plan accordingly. You know enough about school to make effective decisions, whereas last year you were just trying to survive. This is comforting. In your life outside school you are probably very comfortable in the city and do not worry too much about daily living. You have an established social life and tend to do things with a core group of friends rather than the group of new teachers who came with you last year. At this point, it is clear if you are going to stay or leave next year (assuming you have signed a two-year contract). Many schools will ask you to decide by the December break or upon your return.

Teacher Time: First Years Overseas by Kali B.

Since moving overseas in March 2012, I have not once regretted my decision. I've definitely experienced the 5 main stages of living abroad, with only a short amount of time, fortunately, spent in the WTF stage. I've grown to be a more patient and go-with-the-flow person since moving to Poland and now Morocco.

One of the biggest adjustments I've encountered since moving overseas is "Polish Time" or "Moroccan Time". This is where you're given a time frame for something to happen, but it never does. It could take days or weeks longer. While this doesn't necessarily apply to all cultures, it exists in Poland and Morocco. These are societies that aren't plugged in 24/7 like a lot of western cultures, and they'll get to it...eventually. And they do, just not in the instantaneous way that we're use to.

I've never found it difficult to make friends overseas. The other teachers at your school are built-in friends. The first time goodbyes, when the other teachers that have become friends move on to new places, were extremely difficult. But now "goodbyes" have become "see you laters". Those people you've really connected with you'll make an effort to see again.

Sure, there are plenty of things that I don't understand why they're done that way, but that's part of the experience of living in a foreign country. It's much easier to adapt to a new place if you're willing to accept it for what it is rather than complaining about all the things they should change to better fit the lifestyle you're used to. If you want things to be exactly how they were in your home country, then why leave at all?

Kali B. has taught 5th grade in Wroclaw, Poland and currently teaches 4th grade at Casablanca American School in Casablanca, Morocco. She found out about teaching overseas through researching different avenues to move abroad.

Second year. The second year is a period of reflection and discovery. Many second-year teachers spend their breaks traveling. Where you might not have felt comfortable going to a festival or traveling on the weekends, you can now spend your time off the tourist trail discovering quaint festivals, hidden alleys or towns most people do not realize exist. Many first year teachers go back to their home country over the first summer and realize they either missed their overseas school and community or cannot wait to get out. Depending on your contract, you might have decided to move on or stay. This will definitely affect the rest of your year. Regardless, it will be an experience you never forget. You will realize that you can communicate, at least in cafes, restaurants, and shops relatively well. Being fluent is useful but not as important as you thought in the first few months.

Teacher Time: Transitioning your child to an international School by Emily Meadows

As a professional school counselor, I've worked with countless children and families to facilitate their successful transition to an international setting. It can be done! These tips will enhance the experience for your whole family:

- **Routine** – While some of the thrill of moving to an international school is in the newness, remember that children thrive on routine. Keep certain limits the same, such as bedtimes and mealtime expectations, in order to provide your child with a sense of security.

- **Set an Example** – Your child will follow your lead when it comes to embracing something different from what you're used to. Involve your family in the process of exploring this new place, and openly model resilience and a positive attitude when faced with challenge or disappointment.
- **Build Connections** – Support your child in getting to know your new community. Visit the classroom or campus and meet their teachers before the first day of school. Find out if anybody in your housing compound or neighborhood has children around the same age. A sense of personal connection will go a long way in helping your child to feel more at home.
- **Listen** – Children will have their own feelings about the new place. Listen empathically to your child and, though you may not agree, honor their experience by allowing them to share it with you.
- **Play** – Children (yes, even high school students) need to play! Uprooting and moving to a new place can be challenging, and the first year is invariably busy. Make it a priority to carve out play time together as a family. Creating fun memories in your new home is an essential component to making the international school experience one that you and your children will treasure for a lifetime.

Emily Meadows is an alumni of international schools, having attended the Anglo-American School of Moscow and the American School of Paris as a child. Since then, she has built her career as a professional educator and counselor across the world, serving children and families in France, at the American School of Kuwait and, most recently, at Hong Kong International School. She holds a Master of Education degree in Counseling, a Master of Health Science degree in Sexual Health, and is a current Doctor of Philosophy student in Comparative and International Education, researching LGBTQ+ inclusive policy and practice.

10 MOVING

If moving down the block can be compared to a headache, then moving across the world might be compared to a migraine. With some planning, understanding, assistance, and patience a lot of the headache can be eliminated. This chapter outlines the process of moving, followed by different ways you might move to your next school or back to the States.

The most important thing is to plan everything as far in advance as possible. In many cases, it will relieve stress and keep more money in your pocket. Most schools offer some type of help to get you settled and make the transition as easy as possible. By the time you leave, the school may be less likely to help. Many schools today provide at least a nominal amount for moving expenses and a few provide something when you leave. In almost all cases this will not cover all your expenses.

Temporarily or for the Summer

So what do you do with your apartment if you're going to be gone for the winter break or the summer? Thinking ahead can make your vacations much more pleasant. It is important to find someone who is willing to periodically check on your home, make sure everything is there, and water the plants. Finding the right person is important. I have heard horror stories about people inviting their friends to stay in the apartment. Upon returning, they found the person had put thousands of miles on the car and let the bills pile up without paying them. This can lead to stress when you return. I suggest finding someone who will be around all summer, could use a small stipend, and has a long history with the school. In one post, the director's driver was a perfect option while the person who helped staff throughout the year would have been terrible. Another excellent option in some posts is a housekeeper or nanny who will not be working while you are away. This can be written into their contract at the beginning of the year.

The person you leave in charge should have specific duties. I would not suggest having someone do it for free. It would be like asking a lawyer for free advice or asking an acquaintance to move your apartment for you. Although they might do it, they are probably not going to do it very well because there is no motivation. You could pay a stipend to someone based on the number of times they visit your house.

A second option is setting up an exchange with a teacher at another overseas school, a teacher or retired person, or a friend. There are some websites that allow you to post your apartment for rent as well. Take into account that most of your valuables will be in the apartment over the summer and it may not be worth it to rent to complete strangers. I have met teachers who exchange houses with other expatriate teachers for the summer or have a renter pay for the services they use such as the Internet and cable. In my experience, most people end up finding someone to take care of their house while they are away rather than renting it.

Permanently Back to the United States

There are many reasons to move back the United States. A contract might expire, you may be homesick, your parents may need assistance, or you could not find another job overseas. It is important to get a couple of things in order before you go. First, secure transportation of your household effects back to the United States, but have the pickup scheduled close to when you depart. Some people prefer to ship their possessions early. While it is nice to arrive home with your belongings ready to unpack, running to Walmart to buy a few odds and ends is much easier than finishing a school year without the resources you need to live overseas. Most teachers will leave for the States as soon as possible after school ends. It might be somewhat depressing and strange to spend your last week lonely, isolated, and without your belongings. If you don't have something planned, I would suggest leaving with the rest of the staff.

Besides preparing for the move, you need to ensure everything in the host country is in order. In some parts of the world, you must provide written notice to cancel contracts such as cable, Internet, phone, and lease. The penalties for not doing this can be steep. Most schools ask you leave a certain amount of money to cover your final expenses. Schools want you to do this because many have agreements with these companies that provide special benefits (like shorter leases.) If teachers do not pay their bills, the schools may lose these privileges. It's also the right thing to do. Just like moving from the States, you probably have some items to sell. Teachers are vultures when it comes to school supplies and items from your home. Use internal email to post a list of the items you have for sale, the prices, and a photo. Email the new teachers, as well.

School will have an end-of-year checklist of things to do at school before you leave. It is important to get everything on the list done. The business office likely will be your last stop, so you can get paid. It is extremely important to leave your summer contact information. If for nothing else, you will want to receive your tax information.

Teacher Time: Dealing With Shipping Companies Marianne I.

In 2010, we ended our contract with Sana'a International School and moved to Tbilisi, Georgia. In total, we moved 4 people, 6 forty-gallon tubs, 10 suitcases, and a cello. Obviously, taking our swag home for the summer was virtually impossible, which left us with a couple of options. Sometimes your new school will store your belongings if they have the room, but not always. The other option was to locate a shipping company and have them move our house for us. While this may seem daunting at first, shipping your house is a lot easier and more cost effective than the alternatives. There are, however, some important caveats. When you ship your belongings into a foreign country, you will almost always have to pay customs fees. I know this is a total drag (it's your stuff!! Why do you have to pay to ship it in? But you just do, so count on it). In order to assess fees, customs officials need to know what is in your bags. When we shipped our housewares to Georgia, we didn't include a detailed enough packing slip in each bag, and Georgia, unfortunately, is one of those countries that wants a comprehensive list of the contents of each container. So "kitchenware" was nowhere near good enough as a label on our containers. Georgian customs wanted something closer to "10 plates, 25 forks, 6 pans" etc . I cannot emphasize the next bit strongly enough: you need to find out what you cannot bring into the country under any circumstances, and I am not just talking about obvious items like drugs and guns. Some countries will not allow any medication without prescriptions, and bizarrely, this can include vitamin supplements. We didn't know this, so as Georgian customs officials disgorged our poorly labeled bags all over the dusty floor, our school secretary was furtively stuffing our calcium tablets in her purse so that they didn't end up in the trash. In the end, we were charged $500 and all of our neatly packed goods were now covered in dirt and stuffed back into our bags. In 2013, we moved from Los Angeles, California to Karachi, Pakistan. The shipping company was far better than the one we used in Yemen, knew what Pakistani customs would want in terms of paperwork on our goods, and made sure that every container was properly labeled. When the shipment arrived in Pakistan, not one bag was opened, and we were only charged $150 in customs. Work with your old school to find a reputable shipping company, and with your new school to find out about customs requirements and restrictions. Moving is never easy, but it doesn't have to be a horror show, either. Good luck!

Marianne I., Ph.D. is a teacher at the Karachi American School in Karachi, Pakistan

Sudden Move (Breaking Contract)

Unfortunately, sometimes things do not work out. On rare occasions teachers decide to leave before their contract is fulfilled. There might be a serious medical condition, a death in the family, or professional disagreements. Regardless of the reason, the stress of leaving will inevitably increase. Administrators must decide how to replace you and may not be helpful. In some cases, they may be downright difficult. They invested a lot of money and time in you and expected you to finish your contract. A leave of absence is a lot better than simply breaking contract.

This is not a decision to take lightly. Although I heard of a blackball list of teachers who have broken contract, this is probably not true. However, getting another job overseas may prove a 'Herculean' task. Directors talk to each other about potential new hires at conferences and emails. You almost certainly will need to provide the school with a list of past teaching positions. Leaving your overseas schools experience out is not practical and borders on unethical. If you had a medical reason for leaving, that could be useful in explaining your sudden move. Although this is a double-edged sword, it is worth including a short explanation in your cover letter.

A sudden move involves planning and moving quickly. If you broke your contract for personal reasons, the school may not be required to provide any assistance. In that case, you need to pay for your flight home, find a moving company, and close your accounts before leaving. If you have allies in the school, seek their help. In extreme cases, you may need to return to the country at a later time to close out accounts. Finally, you should consider what you are going to do once you move back to the States.

To the Next School

Many overseas teachers decide to move from one school to another every few years. Although I do not have any data on this, I think the average amount of time teachers stay with one school is from three to seven years. In developing countries, the number of years is probably fewer, and more in developed countries. If you are so lucky, you should follow the same procedures as moving back to the United States. Many schools include a shipping allowance for leaving while your next school will provide you with one for getting there. In this case, you will be much closer to covering the costs involved from moving from one host country to another. Some people decide to move their items via a cargo container while others use much smaller methods. Whatever you choose, be prepared to live without your items for at least a few weeks when you arrive at your new post. Many countries have slow customs offices.

Evacuation

In extreme situations, it might be necessary to leave your school, home, and host country in a very short period of time. The two main reasons for leaving are a natural disaster and a political event. It can range from leaving the school and going directly to a plane (unlikely), to having a few hours to get your things together (somewhat unlikely), to a day or two (more likely) to prepare. Your first priority should be safety. Nothing you own should be more important than keeping yourself out of harm's way.

Instead of figuring out the logistics of getting home on a commercial plane or closing accounts, your focus should be on consolidating your most essential items to bring and securing the rest of your belongings. In all situations, your first priority should be getting your important documents, including your passport, and keeping them with you at all times. Hopefully all your documents will be in a safe or in a safe bag at your house or school. From there, fill a second bag or piece of luggage with items you do not want to lose. Consider clothes for at least a few weeks. You may be evacuated to a hotel in another country rather than going back to the United States. Versatile clothes rather than your nicest clothes are more sensible. Unlike normal flights, in evacuation situations your mode of transport out of the evacuation zone may be crowded and chaotic. The evacuation coordinator may only allow you to bring one extra bag. However, pack another with more items just in case.

For items you leave behind, put them in the most secure place you can before leaving. Your school may be the best location especially if it has guards or at least some sort of protection. Ask school personnel if this option is available. Otherwise, pay a local resident to stay at your home to keep a presence and keep intruders out.

Even if a remote possibility exists that something will happen, planning ahead makes sense. Keep important documents together. Have a plan for what you would take with just a carry on, one bag, or two bags. Line up someone to watch your stuff. Ask the school if this has ever happened and how it was handled. Being prepared can make the difference between getting out safely with your most prized possessions and whatever the alternative is.

How much money should you stash for an emergency? At a minimum, I would keep a couple of hundred of U.S. dollars or Euros on hand that can be used to get transportation out of the country. Once you are out of the country it is relatively easy to get cash in most places today. Local currency is okay but it might lose value in an emergency while U.S. dollars or Euros are universally known to be stable and valuable currencies in a crisis.

.

11 OVERSEAS ORGANIZATIONS

All of these organizations have websites that can be easily viewed through an Internet search.

Regional Organizations

Association of American Schools in South America

The Association of American Schools of Central America, Colombia, the Caribbean and Mexico

Association of International Schools in Africa

The Central and Eastern European Schools Association

East Asia Regional Council of Schools

The European Council of International Schools (ECIS)

The Mediterranean Association of International Schools

Near East South Asia Council of Overseas Schools

Department of Defense Education Activity

Overseas Job Sites

Search Associates

International Schools Services

University of Northern Iowa

The International Educator

International Schools Review

Other Helpful Sites

Association for the Advancement of International Education

Office of Overseas Schools

International Baccalaureate

Advanced Placement

Overseas School Research

Institute of International Education

Association for Supervision and Curriculum Development

National Association for Secondary School Principals

Association of Middle Level Education

ISC Research

The International Schools Association

Marzano Research Laboratory

Appendix A: INTERVIEW QUESTIONS RELATED TO OVERSEAS TEACHING

School

1. How do you deal with diversity in the classroom?

2. What experience do you have with English Language Learners?

3. How do you deal with school issues when the answer is not directly available?

4. Are you an independent worker?

5. What (leadership/professional development/curriculum) experience can you contribute to our school?

Living Overseas

6. What experience do you have overseas? Have you traveled overseas in the past?

7. What does your family think about you moving overseas?

8. Why are you applying for this specific school? Position?

9. Where do you see yourself in five years?

10. What do you know about (the host country)? The school?

Appendix B: CONTRACT COMPONENTS

Underlined items are essential. A contract should not be signed if any of the underlined items are not included.

General

- <u>Contract should be on school letterhead</u>
- <u>Contract should be dated</u>
- <u>Contract should be initialed by director, board president, or designated official on every page</u>
- Contract should look and 'feel' legal
- <u>Each clause should be very specific</u> in the interests of the both the school and you. Ask to see policies if they are referenced in the contract.
- <u>There should be a signature by the director, board president, or designated official at the end of the contract</u>
- <u>You should get a signed copy of the contract at the time of signing</u>

Checklist:

- <u>Includes the name of the school, your full name, and the date the contract was written</u>
- Includes information such as your passport number
- <u>Specifies the contract period</u>
- The contract period is usually one calendar year although somewhere the contract should note the actual number of days of employment (e.g. 180 days + five in-service days)
- Indicates a full- or part-time position
- The school's obligations: This might include any of the benefits listed in the section on benefits. The following list includes many of the most common clauses:
- <u>Pay period</u>
- <u>Currency of payment</u>
- <u>Tax obligations by the school and you</u>
- <u>Specific housing benefits</u>

- Retirement benefits
- Dependent's tuition (and fees)
- Be sure to ask about capital fees and other expenses. Capital fees are funds to pay for capital projects like buildings or computer labs. Each family pays somewhere between $2,000-$5,000 although some schools require the payment for each child.
- Visa support
- Airfare to and from the host country*
- Airfreight, cargo, or shipping allotments*
- Professional development
- Health plan*
- Sick leave (should include specific number of days)May include clause about limits after a certain number of sick days has been accrued, how a teacher can 'sell' them back to the school when they leave, or a sick bank
- Personal leave (should include specific number of days)
- Job search leave/Sabbatical leave/Emergency leave/Maternity leave/Paternity leave
- Your obligations
- Number of working days per contract period
- Number of hours you work each day
- Obligations for extracurricular activities
- Professional development
- Up-to-date licensure
- Uniform obligations such as meeting with parents, confidentiality, planning, etc.
- Know and follow school's policies
- Some contracts include a vaguely worded statement about fulfilling any duties tasked by the director or board
- Termination: Each type of termination should indicate when your salary will cease
- Noncompliance with policies
- Reduction in force
- Termination by school or employee
- Sickness
- Closure of school
- Conflict of Interest
- Nepotism
- Financial issues
- Periodic Review by Administration
- Classroom observations

- <u>Teacher access to personnel file</u>

*May not be a part of the contract. However, if they were negotiated or discussed in the interview, they should be in the contract.

Appendix C: SAMPLE EMAIL AND COVER LETTER

Initial Email

Subject: 8th Grade Science Position (2013-2014)

Dear Dr. XXX,

Hello, my name is John Doe and I have been a middle school science teacher for the past ten years. I am interested in applying for the Grade 8 Science position I recently found on your website. With my experience as a classroom teacher, volleyball coach, and student council advisor, I think you will find me to be an exemplary candidate.

I will be attending the XXX fair this February and hope to have a chance to meet you. I am attaching a detailed CV. Please feel free to contact me if you need any more information.

Regards,

John Doe

Cover Letter Attachment

Dear Dr. XXX,

I am writing regarding the 8th grade science position available for the 2013-2014 school year. I think you will find that my experience and talents as an educator make me an excellent candidate. My wife, a school psychologist, and our 3-year-old daughter are also interested in the adventure of moving overseas.

There are a few qualities that might separate me from other candidates. I have ten years of exemplary experience that has included national awards and opportunities to present other teachers. I have participated in many extracurricular activities but have a passion for volleyball. Beyond school, I have traveled extensively in many parts of the world including two years in the Peace Corps.

In a decade of classroom teaching, I have fostered student achievement with rewarding experiences. My framework of teaching is based on the learning-by-doing approach. Students use real-life situations to describe scientific events. This style of teaching led me to receive one of three honorable mentions from the National Science Foundation's Innovative Teachers Award in 2009. In addition, the district superintendent asked me to lead 100 middle school science teachers through a new program developed by the National Committee on Middle School Science Standards. The outcomes revealed that we accomplished all our goals in a timely manner.

Besides teaching, I enjoy being around students outside the classroom. In each of my ten years I have participated in at least two extracurricular activities. As mentioned, my passion is volleyball and I would love to assist with the volleyball program as much as possible. I also have experience with basketball, soccer, wrestling, student council, the Science Olympiad, and as faculty advisor to the district's PTO.

My wife, Jan, is eager to assimilate into a new culture. We met while serving in the Peace Corps and have spent the last twelve years dreaming about moving overseas again. Recently, we decided the time had come as our daughter turned 3 and Jan finished a graduate program in psychology.

Please feel free to contact me at any time via email, johndoe@school.org or my cell phone 555 555 5555.

Regards,

John Doe

8th Grade Science Teacher

johndoe@school.org

555 555 555

Appendix D: SAMPLE RESUME

Kent Matthew Blakeney

2629 Wooster Court Vienna VA 22180

kentblakeney@gmail.com

410 533 5498

Highlights

Ph.D. in
Leadership in
Education

Education

Capella University	2009-2012

Ph.D. in Leadership in Education Administration
- Dissertation "Traditional and Cyber Bullying and Victimization in Overseas Middle Schools"

Walden University	2007-2009
- **M.S. in Education**, focus in technology

Miami University - Oxford, OH	1994-1998
- **B.S. in Education**, Secondary Social Studies
- **B.A. in History**

Administrative/Leadership Experience

Middle School
Coordinator

Instituted
Middle School
Program

MS Coordinator	2015- 2016
- Initiated MS Coordinator position including management and implementation of all new Middle School activities including regular grade level meetings, common agreements, and coordination of special events among 20 staff members and 130 students.
- Designed and established Positive Behavior Support Program, Service Learning Program, and Middle School Success Program.
- Coordinated week long, off campus Week Without Walls program.

Worked with
leadership team
on a variety of
school-wide
initiatives

Administrative Internship	2011-2012
- 360 hours in all areas of leadership.

Chair- Buildings and Grounds Common Areas Committee	2014-2015
- Led to construction of a new campus.

Faculty Representative to the Board	
- Secured equality in pay for faculty | 2013-2014
- Represented faculty at Board meetings and retreats

kentblakeney@gmail.com 410 533 5498

178

Licensure

Certified K-12 Principal

- **K-12 Principal**, State of Minnesota
- **Secondary Social Studies**, State of Kentucky
- **SLLA**, passing score in August 2016

Overseas Teaching Experience

Experience and leadership at six international schools

- **International School of Dakar-Dakar, Senegal** — 2014-2016
- **American School of Antananarivo -Antananarivo, Madagascar** — 2012-2014
- **American International School -Vienna, Austria** — 2009-2012
- **Lincoln School -Kathmandu, Nepal** — 2008-2009
- **Rabat American School -Rabat, Morocco** — 2005-2007
- **American Nicaraguan School -Managua, Nicaragua** — 2004-2005

IB and AP experience and training

Middle and High School experience and leadership

  - Taught IB Economics, IB Geography, AP Macroeconomics, AP European History
  - Taught over ten social studies classes from grades 6 to 12
  - Coached soccer
  - MUN Advisor at three schools

U.S. Teaching Experience

Social Studies, Science, and Math experience

- **Apple Valley Middle School-Hendersonville, North Carolina** — 2001-2003
- **Hunter's Creek Middle School-Jacksonville, North Carolina** — 2000-2001
  - Taught Grade 7 Social Studies and Science
  - Coached soccer and wrestling

Writings/Presentations/Website

Professional writing

- **Dissertation** "An Instrument to Measure Traditional and Cyberbullying and Victimization Behaviors in Overseas Middle Years Students" February 2012
- **European League of Middle Level Educators Conference-** January 2012

Professional speaking

- **European Council of International Schools Administrator's Conference** April 2012
- **International Schools Journal** November 2012
- **Association of International Schools in Africa** March 2015

Professional web presence

- *Teaching Overseas: An Insider's Perspective*
- **Overseas School Research**-Founder

Peace Corps El Sauce, Nicaragua — 2003-2004

Committed and ready to serve

- Taught Environmental Education and initiated teacher training program with three rural schools

kentblakeney@gmail.com 410 533 5498

Appendix E: "The General" Overseas School Survey-TGOSS Teacher Test Pilot

"The General" Overseas School Survey-TGOSS

Teacher Test Pilot

Kent M Blakeney Ph.D.

Overseas School Research

27 January 2016

Introduction

"The General" Overseas School Survey, TGOSS survey was developed through several iterations and peer-reviews over in 2013 and 2014. Unlike many other school satisfaction surveys, the TGOSS has several features that make it ideal for the international school audience. The TGOSS was written the international school in mind. For example, unlike surveys developed for large public school in in the United States, the TGOSS focuses on areas such as after school activities and facilities rather than teacher quality and safety. While these are important, the TGOSS reflects the needs of overseas schools.

The survey design reflects the need of international school. The TGOSS was written with parents, teachers, and students in mind. Each item (question) is written so that item can be analyzed with the responses from the other stakeholders. For example, an item in the Teacher Instruction section asks teachers, "Overall, I am happy with the amount of technology students use at our school." For parents and students the item (question) would change the word students to my child (for parents) and I (for students.) Each item includes language that can be understood by English Language Learners and international parents. As well, the language was purposefully written so each item can be translated into a local language for parents. While it is possible that the translation may not convey the exact sentiment of the English language survey, the overall validity of the survey is increased. In addition, school and respondent demographic items reflect overseas schools. For example, teachers are asked to respond to typical demographic items such as gender, number of years teaching, etc.; however, several items have been included to reflect international school teachers. Nationality, number of years at current school, marital status, children at the school, and location of school are requested.

It is hoped that schools will adopt the TGOSS as their school satisfaction survey due to the advantages it has over other surveys. Data are aggregated for the entire community including teachers, parents, and students. Furthermore, schools can use the survey to find significant differences between different stakeholders within the school. Data can be compared from one year to the next to see if changes that have been made as part of the results of the survey have actually changed. Finally, schools will be able to compare themselves to the world data, regional data, or to similar schools.

Method

Data were collected using the instrument "The General" Overseas School Survey; TGOSS. The instrument includes 42 general items in eight sections (Leadership (8); Communication (5); Guidance (5); Instruction (5); Facilities (5); Academics I (5); Academics II (5); and Additional (4).) In addition, at the end of each section, respondents can include narrative feedback about that section. For example, after the leadership section, a teacher might leave a comment about the role of the Board of Directors in the school. The TGOSS includes four separate surveys; parent in English, parent in local language, teacher, and student. Each survey is designed to be analyzed individually as well as using the data from the aggregate data of all four surveys. The survey is designed to allow for analysis within each survey and with the entire data set from all four surveys. For example, there may be a significant difference on the parent survey using gender as the independent variable, as well a difference between parents (all) and students within the same item.

Data were collected from 69 respondents from December 2, 2015 through December 12. 2015. Participants were acquired initially through the Facebook group, International School Teachers. As well, colleagues with experience at more than one international school at the International School of Dakar were asked to send a link to the survey to colleagues at other international schools. Once the data were collected, the individual responses were examined to find any anomalies that might exist within any of the individual responses. For example, if a respondent answered each item with a one (including the item on bullying which would almost certainly be four or five based on the results of all the other items) would be excluded. This did not happen and all responses were valid.

Once the data was deemed reliable, the analysis of the data could commence. First, demographic data for each item as well as the demographic data were presented in graph and percentage form. Next, each item was analyzed using the demographic data from items 399 to 3991 to determine if any significant differences existed. Due to the number of responses, non-dichotomous responses (both nominal and ordinal) were combined based on the number of responses and knowledge of overseas teachers to create dichotomous variables. For example, the number of years at your current school was divided into two groups, 1-3 years and more than 3 years (the survey included, 4-7 years, 8-15 years, and more than 15 years as other possible responses.) This was based on the assumption that many overseas school teachers sign initial two year contracts. By the time a teacher has been at the school at least three years, the teachers has signed a second contract or is not on their original contract. Item 395 was divided into elementary school (preschool to grade 5) and secondary school (Grade 6 to 12.) Due to the number of responses, teachers that taught across both levels were excluded. Item 396, total number of years teaching, was divided into the following groups; 1-5 years and more than 5 years (6-10 years, 11-15 years, 16-20 years, and more than 20 years) due to the number of responses. Item 397, marital status, was divided into two groups based on the number of responses, married and single. Subjects taught was not analyzed due to individual response rates. Finally, location was divided into a dichotomous variable. The first group represented areas of the world with many less economically developed countries, LEDCs. This included South America, Middle East and North Africa, Sub-saharan Africa, Southwest Asia (Indian Subcontinent, and Southeast Asia. The second group included areas with a higher percentage of more economically developed countries, MEDCs. This included North America, Europe, and East Asia. Respondents that responded with other were excluded and no responses included Central America or the Caribbean, or Australia and the Pacific.

Due to the response rate, (n=69), the data were analyzed in two ways to find significant differences. The data were first analyzed using the means from the original Likert scale from one (completely disagree) to five (completely agree.) As well, an analysis of the data were conducted using means of the the following scale, disagreement (one or two on the Likert Scale) neutral (three on the Likert Scale) and agreement (four and five on the Likert Scale.) Results are categorized in two sections, the original Likert scale with five options (1 to 5) and the revised Likert (options 1 to 3). For this reason, the means of the two analyses are adjusted to reflect the number of options, five for the original Likert scale, and three for the revised data.

Demographic Data

Demographic Teacher

391. What is your gender?

Female	47	67.1%
Male	23	32.9%

392. What is your nationality?

Local (from this country)	1	1.4%
Expatriate (from a different country)	68	97.1%
Other	1	1.4%

393. How many years have you been at this school?

1-3 years	52	74.3%
4-7 years	15	21.4%
8-15 years	2	2.9%
More than 15 years	1	1.4%

395. What grades do you teach? (Please select all that apply)

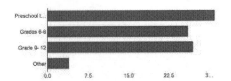

Preschool to Grade 5	31	44.3%
Grades 6-8	26	37.1%
Grade 9- 12	27	38.6%
Other	4	5.7%

396. How many years have you been teaching?

1-5 years	5	7.1%
6-10 years	16	22.9%
11-15 years	23	32.9%
16-20 years	13	18.6%
More than 20 years	13	18.6%

What is your marital status?

Single	23	33.3%
Married	43	62.3%
Other	3	4.3%

398. Do you currently have children at this school?

Yes	26	37.1%
No	44	62.9%

399. What subject(s) do you teach? (Please select all that apply)

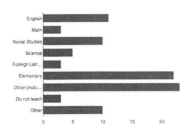

English	11	15.7%
Math	3	4.3%
Social Studies	10	14.3%
Science	5	7.1%
Foreign Language	3	4.3%
Elementary	22	31.4%
Other (including Art, Technology, PE, Drama, etc.)	23	32.9%
Do not teach	3	4.3%
Other	10	14.3%

3991. Where is your current school?

Central America or Carribean	0	0%
South America	1	1.4%
North America	2	2.9%
Europe	7	10.1%
Middle East and Northern Africa	15	21.7%
Sub-Saharan Africa	14	20.3%
Southwest Asia (Indian Subcontinent)	3	4.3%
Southeast Asia	16	23.2%
East Asia	6	8.7%
Australia and Pacfic	0	0%
Other	5	7.2%

187

Leadership

Leaderhip Teacher

311. Overall, I am happy with the leadership at this school.

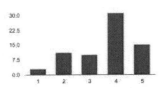

Complete Disagreement: 1	3	4.3%
2	11	15.7%
3	10	14.3%
4	31	44.3%
Complete Agreement: 5	15	21.4%

312. I am happy with the policies in place at the school.

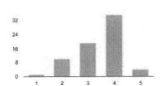

Complete disagreement: 1	1	1.4%
2	10	14.5%
3	19	27.5%
4	35	50.7%
Complete agreement: 5	4	5.8%

313. The Board of Directors is effective in managing the school.

Complete disagreement: 1	10	14.7%
2	7	10.3%
3	17	25%
4	27	39.7%
Complete agreement: 5	7	10.3%

314. The Director/Head of School is effective in his/her job.

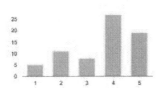

Complete disagreement: 1	5	7.1%
2	11	15.7%
3	8	11.4%
4	27	38.6%
Complete agreement: 5	19	27.1%

315. The Elementary School Principal is effective in his/her job.

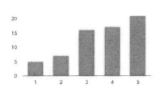

Complete disagreement: 1	5	7.6%
2	7	10.6%
3	16	24.2%
4	17	25.8%
Complete agreement: 5	21	31.8%

316. The Middle School Principal is effective in his/her job.

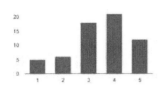

Complete disagreement: 1	5	8.1%
2	6	9.7%
3	18	29%
4	21	33.9%
Complete agreement: 5	12	19.4%

317. The High School Principal is effective in his/her job.

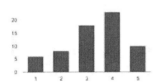

Complete disagreement: 1	6	9.2%
2	8	12.3%
3	18	27.7%
4	23	35.4%
Complete agreement: 5	10	15.4%

Communication

Communication Teacher

321. The school communicates well with me.

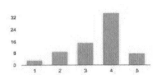

Complete Disagreemnet: 1	3	4.3%
2	9	12.9%
3	15	21.4%
4	35	50%
Complete Agreement: 5	8	11.4%

322. Throughout the year the school has the appropriate number of school events.

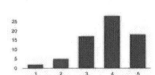
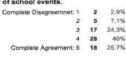

Complete Disagreemnet: 1	2	2.9%
2	5	7.1%
3	17	24.3%
4	28	40%
Complete Agreement: 5	18	25.7%

323. My concerns are dealt with appropriately.

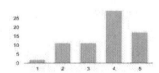

Complete Disagreemnet: 1	2	2.9%
2	11	15.7%
3	11	15.7%
4	29	41.4%
Complete Agreement: 5	17	24.3%

324. The after school activities program is diverse enough to meet the needs of the students.

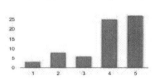

Complete Disagreemnet: 1	3	4.3%
2	8	11.6%
3	6	8.7%
4	25	36.2%
Complete Agreement: 5	27	39.1%

325. I have had good experiences when directly contacting the parents of my students.

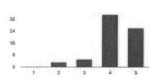

Complete Disagreemnet: 1	0	0%
2	3	4.3%
3	5	7.2%
4	35	50.7%
Complete Agreement: 5	26	37.7%

Guidance

Guidance Teacher

331. Students get help academically when they need it.

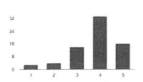

Complete Disagreement: 1	3	4.3%
2	4	5.7%
3	14	20%
4	33	47.1%
Complete Agreement: 5	16	22.9%

332. Children with special needs are supported.

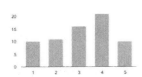

Complete Disagreement: 1	10	14.7%
2	11	16.2%
3	16	23.5%
4	21	30.9%
Complete Agreement: 5	10	14.7%

333. The school's English as a Second Language (ESL) program successfully prepares students for instruction in English.

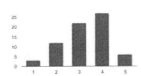

Complete Disagreement: 1	3	4.3%
2	12	17.1%
3	22	31.4%
4	27	38.6%
Complete Agreement: 5	6	8.6%

334. My students will be ready for the next grade at the end of this school year.

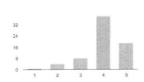

Complete Disagreement: 1	1	1.4%
2	4	5.7%
3	8	11.4%
4	38	54.3%
Complete Agreement: 5	19	27.1%

335. This school teaches students how to be global citizens.

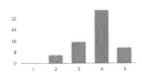

Complete Disagreement: 1	0	0%
2	6	8.6%
3	15	21.4%
4	38	54.3%
Complete Agreement: 5	11	15.7%

Instruction

Instruction Teacher

341. I am happy with the academic progress of the students I teach.

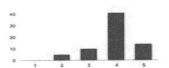

Complete Disagreement: 1	0	0%
2	5	7.1%
3	10	14.3%
4	41	58.6%
Complete Agreement: 5	14	20%

342. Teachers use a variety of up-to-date teaching methods.

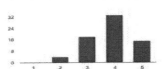

Complete Disagreement: 1	0	0%
2	4	5.7%
3	18	25.7%
4	33	47.1%
Complete Agreement: 5	15	21.4%

343. Overall, I am happy with the amount of technology students use at our school.

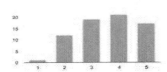

Complete Disagreement: 1	1	1.4%
2	12	17.1%
3	19	27.1%
4	21	30%
Complete Agreement: 5	17	24.3%

344. Overall, I am happy with the classroom resources (textbooks, technology, materials, equipment, etc.)

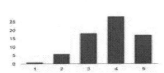

Complete Disagreement: 1	1	1.4%
2	6	8.6%
3	18	25.7%
4	28	40%
Complete Agreement: 5	17	24.3%

345. Overall, I like the school.

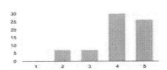

Complete Disagreement: 1	0	0%
2	7	10%
3	7	10%
4	30	42.9%
Complete Agreement: 5	26	37.1%

Facilities

Facilities Teacher

351. Overall, I am happy with the school's facilities.

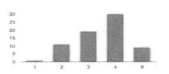

Complete Disagreement: 1	1	1.4%
2	11	15.7%
3	19	27.1%
4	30	42.9%
Complete Agreement: 5	9	12.9%

352. Students are safe at school.

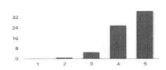

Complete Disagreement: 1	0	0%
2	1	1.4%
3	5	7.2%
4	26	37.7%
Complete Agreement: 5	37	53.6%

353. Buildings at the school are appropriate for learning.

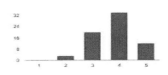

Complete Disagreement: 1	0	0%
2	3	4.3%
3	20	29%
4	34	49.3%
Complete Agreement: 5	12	17.4%

354. Classrooms are the appropriate size for student learning.

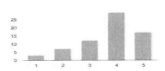

Complete Disagreement: 1	3	4.4%
2	7	10.3%
3	12	17.6%
4	29	42.6%
Complete Agreement: 5	17	25%

355. I am happy with the non-classroom spaces (library, cafeteria, athletic fields, etc.)

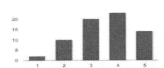

Complete Disagreement: 1	2	2.9%
2	10	14.5%
3	20	29%
4	23	33.3%
Complete Agreement: 5	14	20.3%

Academics I

Academics I Teacher

361. Overall, the school performs well academically.

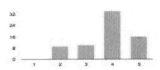

Complete Disagreement: 1	0	0%
2	9	13%
3	10	14.5%
4	34	49.3%
Compete Agreement: 5	16	23.2%

362. Overall, I am happy with the material taught in the classes at this school.

Complete Disagreement: 1	0	0%
2	1	1.4%
3	15	21.4%
4	45	64.3%
Compete Agreement: 5	9	12.9%

363. The school offers a wide selection of classes.

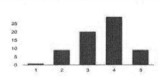

Complete Disagreement: 1	0	0%
2	10	14.7%
3	20	29.4%
4	31	45.6%
Compete Agreement: 5	7	10.3%

364. Students get an appropriate amount of homework each night.

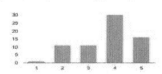

Complete Disagreement: 1	1	1.5%
2	9	13.2%
3	20	29.4%
4	29	42.6%
Compete Agreement: 5	9	13.2%

365. I am happy with the daily schedule of classes and breaks.

Complete Disagreement: 1	1	1.4%
2	11	15.9%
3	11	15.9%
4	30	43.5%
Compete Agreement: 5	16	23.2%

Academics II

Academics II Teacher

371. Students earn good grades.

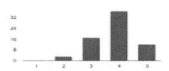

Complete Disagreement: 1	0	0%
2	3	4.3%
3	17	24.6%
4	37	53.6%
Complete Agreement: 5	12	17.4%

372. The school effectively uses collaboration among students.

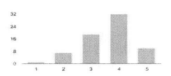

Complete Disagreement: 1	1	1.4%
2	7	10.1%
3	19	27.5%
4	32	46.4%
Complete Agreement: 5	10	14.5%

373. Students know how to conduct research.

Complete Disagreement: 1	3	4.5%
2	14	20.9%
3	28	41.8%
4	16	23.9%
Complete Agreement: 5	6	9%

374. The assessments (test, quizzes, projects, etc.) do a good job of measuring student learning.

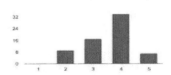

Complete Disagreement: 1	0	0%
2	9	13.4%
3	17	25.4%
4	34	50.7%
Complete Agreement: 5	7	10.4%

375. Students are well behaved.

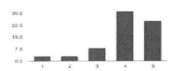

Complete Disagreement: 1	3	4.3%
2	3	4.3%
3	8	11.4%
4	31	44.3%
Complete Agreement: 5	25	35.7%

381. This school provides parents with the appropriate amount of opportunities to volunteer at school.

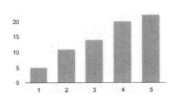

Complete Disagreement: 1	5	6.9%
2	11	15.3%
3	14	19.4%
4	20	27.8%
Complete Agreement: 5	22	30.6%

382. Bullying occurs at this school.

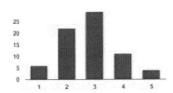

Complete Disagreement: 1	6	8.3%
2	22	30.6%
3	29	40.3%
4	11	15.3%
Complete Agreement: 5	4	5.6%

383. Students are generally happy.

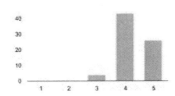

Complete Disagreement: 1	0	0%
2	0	0%
3	4	5.5%
4	43	58.9%
Complete Agreement: 5	26	35.6%

384. Teachers work together at this school.

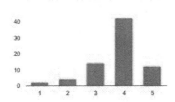

Complete Disagreement: 1	2	2.7%
2	4	5.4%
3	14	18.9%
4	42	56.8%
Complete Agreement: 5	12	16.2%

Additional Teacher

Additional Teacher

361. This school provides parents with the appropriate amount of opportunities to volunteer at school.

Complete Disagreement: 1	5	7.4%
2	11	16.2%
3	13	19.1%
4	18	26.5%
Complete Agreement: 5	21	30.9%

382. Bullying occurs at this school.

Complete Disagreement: 1	6	8.8%
2	20	29.4%
3	27	39.7%
4	11	16.2%
Complete Agreement: 5	4	5.9%

383. Students are generally happy.

Complete Disagreement: 1	0	0%
2	0	0%
3	4	5.8%
4	40	58%
Complete Agreement: 5	25	36.2%

384. Teachers work together at this school.

Complete Disagreement: 1	2	2.9%
2	4	5.7%
3	14	20%
4	38	54.3%
Complete Agreement: 5	12	17.1%

Please Note: Item 382 expected Complete Disagreement to the most positive response.

Descriptive Statistics					
Variable	N	Min	Max	Mean	Std. Dev.
311. Overall, I am happy with the leadership at this school.	69	1	5	3.67	1.080
312. I am happy with the policies in place at the school.	68	1	5	3.47	.855
313. The Board of Directors is effective in managing the school.	67	1	5	3.24	1.195
314. The Director/Head of School is effective in his/her job.	69	1	5	3.65	1.235
315. The Elementary School Principal is effective in his/her job.	65	1	5	3.63	1.257
316. The Middle School Principal is effective in his/her job.	61	1	5	3.46	1.163
317. The High School Principal is effective in his/her job.	64	1	5	3.38	1.162
321. The school communicates well with me.	69	1	5	3.54	.994
322. Throughout the year the school has the appropriate number of school events.	69	1	5	3.78	1.013

323. My concerns are dealt with appropriately.	69	1	5	3.71	1.086
324. The after school activities program is diverse enough to meet the needs of the students.	68	1	5	3.93	1.163
325. I have had good experiences when directly contacting the parents of my students.	68	2	5	4.24	.755
331. Students get help academically when they need it.	69	1	5	3.78	1.013
332. Children with special needs are supported.	67	1	5	3.18	1.266
333. The school's English as a Second Language (ESL) program successfully prepares students for instruction in English.	69	1	5	3.32	.993
334. My students will be ready for the next grade at the end of this school year.	69	1	5	4.00	.874
335. This school teaches students how to be global citizens.	69	2	5	3.80	.797
341. I am happy with the academic progress of the students I teach.	69	2	5	3.94	.765
342. Teachers use a variety of up-to-date teaching methods.	69	2	5	3.86	.827
343. Overall, I am happy with the amount of technology students use at our school.	69	2	5	3.62	1.045
344. Overall, I am happy with the classroom resources (textbooks,	69	1	5	3.77	.972

technology, materials, equipment, etc.)				
345. Overall, I like the school.	69	2	5	4.07	.944
351. Overall, I am happy with the school's facilities.	69	1	5	3.49	.964
352. Students are safe at school.	68	2	5	4.46	.679
353. Buildings at the school are appropriate for learning.	68	2	5	3.79	.783
354. Classrooms are the appropriate size for student learning.	67	1	5	3.73	1.095
355. I am happy with the non-classroom spaces (library, cafeteria, athletic fields, etc.)	68	1	5	3.56	1.056
361. Overall, the school performs well academically.	68	2	5	3.82	.945
362. Overall, I am happy with the material taught in the classes at this school.	69	2	5	3.88	.631
363. The school offers a wide selection of classes.	67	2	5	3.51	.877
364. Students get an appropriate amount of homework each night.	67	1	5	3.54	.943
365. I am happy with the daily schedule of classes and breaks.	68	1	5	3.72	1.049
371. Students earn good grades.	68	2	5	3.87	.731

372. The school effectively uses collaboration among students.	68	1	5	3.65	.894
373. Students know how to conduct research.	66	1	5	3.14	.991
374. The assessments (test, quizzes, projects, etc.) do a good job of measuring student learning.	66	2	5	3.61	.839
375. Students are well behaved.	69	1	5	4.01	1.022
381. This school provides parents with the appropriate amount of opportunities to volunteer at school.	67	1	5	3.60	1.280
382. Bullying occurs at this school.	67	1	5	2.79	1.008
383. Students are generally happy.	68	3	5	4.29	.575
384. Teachers work together at this school.	69	1	5	3.81	.845

Significant Differences

- Regarding gender, females respond more positively to questions about working together and collaboration.
- Regarding years at school, teachers with more than three years at school responded more positively to the questions about the appropriateness of the building and classroom material.
- Regarding years at school, teachers with one to three years at school responded more positively to the question about the academic progress of the students they taught.
- Regarding total number of year teaching, teachers with more than five years of teaching experience responded more positively to the question about student behavior.
- Regarding children at school, teachers with children at the school responded more positively to the questions about liking the school overall and the effectiveness of the head of school.
- Regarding children at school, teachers without children at the school responded more positively to the questions about the diversity of the after school programs, the happiness of the students, and (incidences of) bullying.
- Regarding development, teachers from regions from more economically developed countries, responded more positively to the questions about the effectiveness of the head of school, the amount of homework given to students, and communication.

Variable	Item	Likert Scale	Higher Response
Gender	384. Teachers work together at this school.	5 point	Female

	372. The school effectively uses collaboration among students.	3 point	Female
	384. Teachers work together at this school	3 point	Female
Years at School	353. Buildings at the school are appropriate for learning	5 point	More than 3 Years
	341. I am happy with the academic progress of the students I teach.	3 point	1-3 Years
	344. Overall, I am happy with the classroom resources (textbooks, technology, materials, equipment, etc.)	3 point	More than 3 Years
	353. Buildings at the school are appropriate for learning.	3 point	More than 3 Years
Number of Years Teaching	375. Students are well behaved.	3 point	More than 5 Years
Children at School	324. The after school activities program is diverse enough to meet the needs of the students.	5 point	No Children at School
	345. Overall, I like the school.	5 point	Children at School
	383. Students are generally happy.	5 point	No Children at School
	314. The Director/Head of School is effective in his/her	3 Point Likert	Children at School

	job.		
	382. Bullying occurs at this school.	3 Point	No Children at School
	383. Students are generally happy.	3 Point	No Children at School
Development	314. The Director/Head of School is effective in his/her job.	5 point	MEDCs
	364. Students get an appropriate amount of homework each night.	5 point	MEDCs
	314. The Director/Head of School is effective in his/her job.	3 Point	MEDCs
	321. The school communicates well with me.	3 Point	MEDCs

Notes: Higher response rate indicates the variable that had more positive responses. For example, more females than males indicated that teachers work together; MEDC- more economically developed countries; LEDC- less economically developed countries

ABOUT THE AUTHOR

Kent Blakeney has been an overseas educator since 2003. He has taught middle school and high school social studies, science, and math in North Carolina, Nicaragua, Morocco, Nepal, Austria, Madagascar, and Senegal. Kent has a Bachelor of Science in Secondary Education and a Bachelor of Arts in History from Miami University of Ohio, a Master's in Education from Walden University, and a PhD in Educational Leadership from Capella University. Kent is also the founder of Overseas School Research. When not teaching, Kent likes to spend time with his two children and wife, play golf, run, read, and spend time in the backcountry. Kent currently lives and teaches in Dakar, Senegal. He can be reached at kentblakeney@gmail.com.

57648163R00120

Made in the USA
Lexington, KY
21 November 2016